TORAH PORTIONS FOR CHILDREN
BaMidbar
BOOK 4: NUMBERS

NATALEE HENRY & YEVGENIYA CALENDRILLO

TORAH PORTIONS FOR CHILDREN
BaMidbar
BOOK 4: NUMBERS

Natalee Henry & Yevgeniya Calendrillo

Copyright © Natalee Henry & Yevgeniya Calendrillo, 2024.

Printed in the United States 2024.

All rights reserved. This book may not be copied or reprinted for commercial gain or profit. No portion of this book may be reproduced, stored in a retrieval system, transmitted in any form or by any means electronic, mechanical photocopy, recording, or any other except brief quotations in printed reviews, without the prior permission of the Authors and the Publisher. Rights for publishing this book in other languages are to be in written permission by Natalee Henry and Yevgeniya Calendrillo.

Unless otherwise stated, scripture References are from the New American Standard Bible (NASB), and the Tree of Life Version.

This book is a part of the Torah for Children Curriculum. www.torah4children.net

ISBN 978-1-66640-578-1

Acknowledgments

Thanks to Ken & Lisa Albin, our Family, and Tribe at Save The Nations for your continued love, support, and encouragement throughout our writing journey.

Special thanks to Kiwi Gomes for editing, Tammie Taylor for proofreading, and all the teachers at Save The Nations who have been serving in the children's ministry teaching this curriculum.

Torah Portion Titles

1. BaMidbar - In The Wilderness   Page 1
2. Nasso - Lift Up   Page 18
3. Beha'Alotcha - When You Set Up   Page 35
4. Shelach Lecha - Send On Your Behalf   Page 52
5. Korach - Bald   Page 70
6. Chukkat - Statute*   Page 88
7. Balak - Balak*   Page 88
8. Pinchas - Phinehas   Page 107
9. Mattot - Tribes*   Page 124
10. Massei - Journeys*   Page 124

About the Authors   Page 143
About the Book   Page 145

* Indicates that these two Torah Portions are read separately during a leap year but are combined during a regular calendar year.

*NOTE TO TEACHERS/PARENTS:

Dear Teachers and Parents,

Thank you for choosing to help us equip our children in the Torah Way of the Messiah. We are grateful for you and your time of service.

Each lesson is designed as a guide for teaching the Torah Portions. We encourage you to review the lesson in advance to become familiar with the material provided and allow the Holy Spirit to give you insights for teaching the lesson.

Each lesson is structured so our children will learn from the Torah Portions, see the connection with Yeshua (Jesus), and understand the work of the Holy Spirit. Our aim is not just to give information but to teach Torah principles and demonstrate how to use them in their lives.

Every lesson has a general summary of the Torah Portion for the teachers and a lesson summary for the main lesson you will teach for the Torah Portion. With each lesson, there are practical applications and questions. The questions are given at the end of the lesson, however, the teacher can incorporate the questions at any time during the lesson. The practical applications are a great way for the children to make the connection between Torah and their everyday lives.

Thanks again for your time and service in helping to equip our children in the Torah Way of the Messiah.

SUGGESTED CLASS SCHEDULE

Welcome

Practical Application Follow-up From the Last Lesson *(See the Practical Application Page)*

Torah Portion Lesson

Bathroom Break

Crafts

Snacks

LESSON CONTENTS

Torah Portion Name and Meaning
Torah Portion Theme
Torah Portion Outline
Lesson
    Title and Meaning
    Scriptures
    Theme
    Summary
    Lesson Discussion
    Turning Point *(THIS SECTION IS FOR CHILDREN 9 AND OLDER)*
Practical Applications
Questions and Answer Sheet
Crafts and Instructions

BaMidbar

"In The Wilderness"

Torah Portion 34: BaMidbar "In The Wilderness"

The Title of this week's Torah portion is **"BaMidbar"**. It is the Hebrew word that is translated as **"in the wilderness."** It is found in the first verse of our Torah reading.

Numbers 1:1
Now the Lord spoke to Moses **in the wilderness** of Sinai, in the tent of meeting, on the first day of the second month, in the second year after they had come out of the land of Egypt, saying,

Scripture Readings:
Numbers 1:1-4:20, 1 Samuel 20:18-42, Matthew 24:29-36, Psalm 122

The Theme of the Torah Portion:

Numbering of the people in the camp

Scripture for Theme

Numbers 1:19 NASB

Just as the Lord had commanded Moses. So he numbered them in the wilderness of Sinai.

Torah Portion Outline

- The Command to Number the People, **Numbers 1:1-4**
- Leaders Chosen by Adonai, **Numbers 1:5-19**
- Men Counted for Military, **Numbers 1:20-43**
- Don't Count the Levites, **Numbers 1:44-54**
- Encampment of the Tribes, **Numbers 2:1-2**
- Tribes Camped on the East Side, **Numbers 2:3-9**
- Tribes that Camped on the South Side, **Numbers 2:10-16**
- The Tent of Meeting and the Levites, **Numbers 2:17**
- Tribes Camped on the West Side, **Numbers 2:18-24**
- Tribes Camped on the North Side, **Numbers 2:25-31**
- Total Number of People in the Camps, **Numbers 2:32-34**
- Descendants of Aaron and Moses, **Numbers 3:1-5**
- The tribe of Levi was Assigned to Help Aaron, **Numbers 3:6-13**
- Counting of the Tribe of Levi, **Numbers 3:14-39**
- Registration of all the Firstborn Males, **Numbers 3:40-43**
- Levites were Chosen as Firstborn to Adonai, **Numbers 3:44-51**

- Counting the Descendants of Kohath, **Numbers 4:1-3**
- Duties for the Descendants of Kohath, **Numbers 4:4-15**
- Duties for Eleazar, **Numbers 4:17**
- Protection for the Descendants of Kohath, **Numbers 4:18-20**

LESSON SUMMARY

Two years after God delivered the children of Israel out of Egypt, He commanded Moses to count the people. He told Moses to assemble all the people and count them by their tribe and families. Moses was told to record the names of all the men twenty years and older who were to serve in the military. He was also told to take with him, Aaron, and the leaders from each clan to help him count the people. Adonai gave him a list of names of men from each tribe, whom He chose as leaders. Moses, Aaron, and the twelve leaders counted the men as Adonai commanded. The tribe of Levi was not counted because they were not allowed to serve in the military. The total number of men counted for military service from the tribes was 603,550.

Adonai gave orders for how the tribes should camp around the Tabernacle. In each camp, there were three tribes. Only one tribe was assigned as leader of each camp around the Tabernacle. Every tribe had its own banner and symbol. They were to set up camp with their banner and symbol. Judah, Issachar, and Zebulon camped together on the east side facing the rising of the sun. Judah was the leader of the camp, with his banner and symbol. The total number in Judah's camp was 186,400 and they were the first to move. The tribe in Reuben's camp under his symbol and banner were: Reuben, Simeon, and Gad. They had 151,450 people in their camp. They were the second to move, and they camped on the south side. After the first two camps moved, then the tribe of Levi would follow with the Tent of Meeting and all its furniture. The camp on the west was under Ephraim's banner and symbol. They were the third camp to move. In this camp were the tribes of Ephraim, Manasseh, and Benjamin. Their total number was 108,100. The last tribes to set out were under the banner of Dan. They camped in the north. Their total number was 157,600 and were from the tribes of Dan, Asher, and Naphtali.

The Levites were not counted for war but chosen as the firstborn to serve as priests. The Levites were in charge of the Tabernacle and all its furniture. Their duties were to set up and take down the tabernacle each time the camp moved to a new location. The Levites were counted and consecrated as firstborn to Adonai. They were chosen instead of all the firstborn males in Israel. Duties were assigned to the three sons of Levi: Gershon, Kohath, and Merari to help Aaron and his sons. The sons of Kohath among the Levites were counted from the age of thirty years old to fifty years old. They served in ministry to do work in the Tent of Meeting. Their duties were caring for the holy things. Duties for Eliazar the priest included: the oil for the Menorah, the fragrance incense, the continual grain offering, and the anointing oil. He also had other duties in the Tabernacle.

LESSON DISCUSSION

Numbers 1: 1-4
Then the Lord spoke to Moses in the wilderness of Sinai, in the tent of meeting, on the first of the second month, in the second year after they had come out of the land of Egypt, saying, **2** "Take a census of all the congregation of the sons of Israel, by their families, by their fathers' households, according to the number of names, every male, head by head **3** from twenty years old and upward, whoever is able to go out to war in Israel, you and Aaron shall number them by their armies. **4** With you, moreover, there shall be a man of each tribe, each one head of his father's household.

Adonai commanded Moses to count the men in Israel. He knew Moses could not count all the men by himself. Adonai chose twelve men, one from each tribe, as leaders to assist Moses and Aaron. They were to count all the men from twenty years old and older for war. The total number counted from all the tribes was 603,550.

God always has someone to help us do what He asked us to do.

Adonai chose twelve men, one from each tribe, to help Moses and Aaron count the men for war. Yeshua chose twelve disciples to help Him spread the Good News of the Kingdom while He was on earth.

Luke 6:12-13
And it was during these days that Yeshua went out to the mountain to pray, and He spent all night in prayer to God. **13** When day came, He called His disciples, choosing from among them twelve whom He also named emissaries

Adonai, our Heavenly Father, sent the Holy Spirit (Ruach HaKodesh) to help us be His disciples. The Ruach gives us boldness and power to tell others about Yeshua and His Kingdom.

1 Corinthians 12: 4-11 Message

God's various gifts are handed out everywhere; but they all originate in God's Spirit. God's various ministries are carried out everywhere; but they all originate in God's Spirit. God's various expressions of power are in action everywhere; but God himself is behind everything. Each person is given something to do that shows who God is; everyone gets in on it, and everyone benefits. All kinds of things are handed out by God's Spirit, and to all kinds of people! The variety is wonderful: wise counsel, clear understanding, simple trust, healing the sick, miraculous acts, proclamation, distinguishing between spirits, tongues, and interpretation of tongues. All these gifts have a common origin, but are handed out by the Spirit of God one by one. He decides who gets what, and when.

Every tribe had its duties. They were assigned a place around the Tabernacle. They received instructions for the order each tribe moved to travel through the wilderness. Adonai led them as they traveled through the wilderness. Even the Levites had their specific duties as they served as priests to help Aaron. No one was allowed to do whatever they wanted and still lived in the community of Israel. They had to work together to serve Adonai and obey His commands.

Numbers 2:32-34

These are the numbered men of the sons of Israel by their fathers' households; the total of the numbered men of the camps by their armies, 603,550. **33** The Levites, however, were not numbered among the sons of Israel, just as the Lord had commanded Moses. **34** Thus the sons of Israel did; according to all that the Lord commanded Moses, so they camped by their standards, and so they set out, every one by his family according to his father's household.

Each of us also has a special place and assignment in God's Kingdom. God also has people who will help us with His assignment. We all have different assignments but we must all work together for God's purpose.

1 Corinthians 3:8-9 TLV

Now he who plants and he who waters work as one, but each will receive his own reward according to his own labor. **9** For we are God's co-workers; you are God's field, God's building.

TURNING POINT:

DESIGNATED FOR PURPOSE

Numbers 1:17-19

So Moses and Aaron took these men who had been designated by name, **18** and they assembled all the congregation together on the first of the second month. Then they registered by ancestry in their families, by their fathers' households, according to the number of names, from twenty years old and upward, head by head, **19** just as the Lord had commanded Moses. So he numbered them in the wilderness of Sinai.

It had been a little over two years since Adonai chose Moses to lead the children of Israel out of Egypt. From the beginning, God had assigned others to help him. Moses was not confident in his speech to go before Pharaoh so Adonai sent Aaron his brother to speak for him. Their sister Miriam also proved to be a great help to them once they crossed the Reed Sea. Adonai used Jethro, Moses' father-in-law, to give him wise counsel. He told Moses to appoint leaders from among the people to help him with the daily affairs of the people (Exodus 18).

Joshua became Moses' assistant. The Levites showed excellent leadership. They helped Moses defend the honor of Adonai after Aaron made the golden calf for the people to worship. This is the reason Adonai chose them to serve as priests to Aaron instead of the firstborn in Israel.

After Adonai gave Moses instructions to build the Tabernacle, all its furnishings, and the priestly garments, He then designated men with skills and wisdom to do the work. In this week's Torah portion, Adonai also designated men to help Moses and Aaron count the men for military service.

Moses was Adonai's chosen prophet. There is no other prophet in the Tanach (Old Testament) with whom Adonai spoke face to face (Numbers 12:6-8). As we reflect on Moses we see he was not alone on his journey to bring the children of Israel to the promised land. Adonai appointed people at different stages of his journey to help him. Moses recognized his need for Adonai and also for people to help (Numbers 11:14).

We can learn from the life of Moses that Adonai will always send others to help us with the assignment He has given us. Begin to pray and ask Adonai to reveal to you His assignment for your life. Ask Him to prepare you for your assignment and for the people He will assign to help you along the way. May you learn to hear the voice of Adonai and obey as He speaks.

PRACTICAL APPLICATIONS

FOR CHILDREN 4-6 YEARS OLD
Practice being a good helper for your parents.

FOR CHILDREN 7-12 YEARS OLD
Pray and ask God to show you where you can be of help to someone. Also, if you need help with school, or having a difficult time with someone, ask Him to send you the right people who can help you.

FOLLOW-UP FROM THE LAST TORAH PORTION
Ask who wants to share from last week's practical application
FOR CHILDREN 4-6 YEARS OLD
Put away your favorite toys for the next 7 days.

FOR CHILDREN 7-12 YEARS OLD

LEARN TO SPEAK A BLESSING OTHERS
Ask your family members or friends if they follow God's commands. If they answer yes, then say, **"May the Lord bless you and keep you!"**
If they answer no, then ask, "Would you like to pray and ask God to forgive your sins and accept Yeshua?"

QUESTIONS - TEACHERS ANSWER KEY

1. **How many camps were set up around the Tabernacle?**
   Four (4)

2. **At what age were the men counted for the military?**
   Twenty (20) and older

3. **How many leaders did Adonai choose to assist Moses and Aaron?**
   Twelve (12), one from each tribe

4. **Which tribe was not counted for the military?**
   Levi

5. **What was the total number of men counted?**
   603,550

6. **Name the tribes that camped on the east side of the Tabernacle.**
   Judah, Issachar, Zebulun

7. **Which tribe was redeemed as firstborn to Adonai?**
   Levi

8. **Name the tribes camped on the west side of the Tabernacle.**
   Ephraim, Manasseh, Benjamin

9. **Which of Levi's sons was chosen to serve in ministry and help Aaron?**
   Kohath

10. **Which tribes were in Reuben's camp on the south side of the Tabernacle?**
    Reuben, Simeon, Gad

11. **Which tribes camped on the north side of the Tabernacle?**
    Dan, Asher, Naphtali

QUESTIONS - CHILDREN'S COPY

1. How many camps were set up around the Tabernacle?

2. At what age were the men counted for the military?

3. How many leaders did Adonai choose to assist Moses and Aaron?

4. Which tribe was not counted for the military?

5. What was the total number of men counted?

6. Name the tribes that camped on the east side of the Tabernacle.

7. Which tribe was redeemed as firstborn to Adonai?

8. Name the tribes camped on the west side of the Tabernacle.

9. Which of Levi's sons was chosen to serve in ministry and help Aaron?

10. Which tribes were in Reuben's camp on the south side of the Tabernacle?

11. Which tribes camped on the north side of the Tabernacle?

CRAFTS SUPPLIES FOR THE TORAH PORTION BAMIDBAR

SUPPLIES:
1. Popsicle Sticks
2. Double-sided Tape or Glue
3. Print Paper
4. Markers/Pencils

CRAFTS:

1. Distribute to children 12 pre-cut tribe flags.
2. Children will color them. Encourage them to color the background in pencil lightly, so you can still read the tribe names.

3. Children will stick the flags to the "poles" aka popsicle sticks.
4. Color the sticks themselves if time allows.

5. If there's extra time, let Children group the tribes as listed in Numbers 1, and place them east/south/north/west.

Naso
"Lift Up"

Torah Portion 35: Naso "Lift Up"

The Title of this week's Torah portion is Naso. It is from the Hebrew word **"Nasa"** which means **"to lift, lift up, take, or count"**, and it is found in the second verse of our Torah reading.

Numbers 4:21-22

Again Adonai spoke to Moses saying, **22 "Take** a census also of the sons of Gershon, by their ancestral households and by their families.

Scripture Readings:
Numbers 4:21-7:89, Judges 13:2-25, Luke 1:11-20, Psalm 67

The Theme of the Torah Portion:

A Work and a Burden to Carry

Scripture for Theme

Numbers 4:49

From the mouth of Adonai by Moses's hand, each man was assigned his work and his burden to carry. So they were counted, as Adonai commanded Moses.

Torah Portion Outline

- Command to Lift up the Sons of Levi, **Numbers 4:21-23**
- Responsibilities of the Gershonites, **Numbers 4:24-29**
- Responsibilities of the Merarites, **Numbers 4:30-37**
- The Total Number of Sons Counted for Service, **Numbers 4:38-49**
- Purification in the Camp, **Numbers 5:1-4**
- Stealing from a brother or Stranger, **Numbers 5:5-10**
- The Jealous Husband and Sotah Law, **Numbers 5:11-29**
- The Nazarite Vow, **Numbers 6:1-8**
- Unexpected Contamination as a Nazarite, **Numbers 6:9-12**
- Completing Your Nazarite Vow, **Numbers 6:13-22**
- The Priestly Blessing, **Numbers 6:22-27**
- The Tribal Leaders Offerings, **Numbers 7:1-89**

LESSON SUMMARY

This week's Torah portion is a continuation of the previous Torah portion, Bamidbar. At the end of Bamidbar Moses, Aaron, and the Tribal leaders received the command to count the sons of Levi. The sons of Levi - Gershon, Kohath, and Merari - served as priests to Aaron and his sons. Our Torah portion outlines the duties and responsibilities of these sons. Also, the number of men counted from the sons of Levi according to their father's house. Moses was commanded to count the males from 30 to 50 years. Each son was given different tasks, duties, responsibilities, and assignments for the service of the Tabernacle.

Everyone was responsible for maintaining the purity of the camp. Every contaminated person was sent outside the camp. Whoever sinned and broke faith with Adonai, needed to confess their sin, needed to make an apology to the person they had wronged, and needed to ask God for forgiveness. They were to also bring an offering to the priest for him to make atonement on their behalf.

If a man became jealous of his wife, he was to take his concern to the priest. If his wife agreed, then the priest would perform a ritual known as the "Sotah Trial," also known as "Bitter Water," to appease her husband. If the woman was found guilty of being unfaithful to her husband she would not be able to bear children. If she was not guilty she would be able to conceive and bear children.

Specific instructions were also given to anyone who desired to make a Nazarite vow. A Nazarite is someone who desires to separate himself/herself from living an ordinary life. A Nazarite devotes oneself to Adonai for a specific time. The person was to abstain from wine and other strong drinks, was not permitted to eat grapes or raisins, and during the days of his vow, he was not permitted to shave his head or come in contact with a dead body. He was also given instructions should someone die suddenly in his presence. At the end of his vow, he was to present an offering to Adona.

Adonai also gave Moses instructions for when Aaron was to bless the people. Our Torah portion ends with the offerings brought to Adonai for the service of the Tabernacle and to the priest by the twelve tribal leaders. Each tribe brought the same offering each day. They brought their offering in order of their encampment around the Tabernacle.

LESSON DISCUSSION

DUTIES AND ASSIGNMENTS

Everyone had a duty and an assignment that was given to them by Adonai. In the Torah portion Bamidbar; the tribes counted were given specific tasks and duties in their camps around the Tabernacle. In this Torah portion, Naso, Adonai assigned the duties and responsibilities of the sons of Levi for the service of the Tabernacle.

The sons of Gershon — Numbers 4:24-26; This is the task of the Gershonite families in working and carrying burdens. **25** They are to carry the curtains of the Tabernacle, the Tent of Meeting, its covering, the outer covering of porpoise hide, the curtains for the entrance for the Tent of Meeting, **26** the curtains surrounding the courtyard and the altar, the curtain for the entrance, the ropes and all the equipment used in its operations. They are to do all that needs to be done with these things.

The sons of Merari — Numbers 4:31-32; This is their task in the service of the Tent of Meeting: the frames of the Tabernacle, its crossbars, posts and bases, **32** as well as the posts of the surrounding courtyard, plus their bases, tent pegs, ropes, and all their paraphernalia with everything related to their operation. Assign to them by name their duties and tasks.

The Sons of Kohath — Numbers 4:34-37; So Moses, Aaron and the princes of the community counted the sons of the Kohathites according to their families and their ancestral households. **35** All the men who came to do the service of the Tent of Meeting, from 30 to 50 years of age, **36** were counted by families—2,750. **37** This was the total of those in the families of the Kohathites, every one serving in the Tent of Meeting—Moses and Aaron counted them according to the mouth of ADONAI by Moses's hand. The responsibility of the sons of Kohath was to carry the holy items on their shoulders, (Numbers 7:9)

WHAT CAN WE LEARN FROM THIS TORAH PORTION?
1. We are all unique to God.
2. We all have different assignments and duties in the Kingdom of God.
3. Though our duties and assignments are different we must work together to fulfill God's Kingdom Purpose.
4. Our purpose in God's Kingdom is to help each other.
5. When we are obedient, do our duties, and responsibilities, and help each other, we carry the Name of God with us.

THE BLESSING:

NUMBERS 6:22-27 WEB (World English Bible)
And the Lord spoke to Moses, saying: **23** "Speak to Aaron and his sons, saying, 'This is the way you shall bless the children of Israel. Say to them: **24** "The Lord bless you and keep you; **25** The Lord make His face shine upon you, And be gracious to you; **26** The Lord lift up His countenance upon you, And give you peace." '**27** "So they shall put My name on the children of Israel, and I will bless them."

As we walk in obedience to God's word, we walk in His blessing and He puts His name on us.

How do you know if what you are doing is pleasing to God? Ask yourself, "Would God put His Name on what I am doing?

Yeshua walked according to the word of God. He carried out His duties and responsibilities. Because He was obedient, you and I can have a relationship with our Heavenly Father. Before Yeshua was betrayed and arrested, He took three of His disciples with Him to the Mount of Olives to pray. He knew that it was time for Him to die, but it was still painful for Him. In Luke chapter 22, He prayed earnestly for His Father not to let Him die. Yeshua felt the pain of death, but He said, Father, not My will, but Yours be done.

Luke 22:39-43

And He came out and went, as was His habit, to the Mount of Olives; and the disciples also followed Him. **40** Now when He arrived at the place, He said to them, "Pray that you do not come into temptation." **41** And He withdrew from them about a stone's throw, and He knelt down and began to pray, **42** saying, "Father, if You are willing, remove this cup from Me; yet not My will, but Yours be done." **43** Now an angel from heaven appeared to Him, strengthening Him.

TURNING POINT:

A Gift To Adonai

Have you ever received the same gift twice from two different people? Imagine receiving the same gift twelve times!

How would you respond? In our Torah portion, we learn about the gifts that the leaders of Israel brought to Adonai. Each leader brought the same gift.

Number 7:1-6,10-11 NASB2020
"Now on the day that Moses had finished setting up the tabernacle, he anointed it and consecrated it with all its furnishings, and the altar and all its utensils; he anointed them and consecrated them also. **2** Then the leaders of Israel, the heads of their fathers' households, made an offering (they were the leaders of the tribes; they were the supervisors over the numbered men). **3** When they brought their offering before the Lord, six covered carts and twelve oxen, a cart for every two of the leaders and an ox for each one, then they presented them in front of the tabernacle. **4** Then the Lord spoke to Moses, saying, **5** "Accept these things from them, that they may be used in the service of the tent of meeting, and you shall give them to the Levites, to each man according to his service." **6** So Moses took the carts and the oxen and gave them to the Levites." **10** "And the leaders offered the dedication offering for the altar when it was anointed, so the leaders offered their offering before the altar. **11** Then the Lord said to Moses, "They shall present their offering, one leader each day, for the dedication of the altar."

The Leaders brought their gifts to Adonai. Each leader from every tribe presented the same gifts. In our Torah portion, Adonai mentions the gifts and the tribes, as each leader brought their tribes' gift on their day to Adonai.

Why is the giving of gifts mentioned even though they are the same for each tribe? Adonai wanted to teach the children of Israel that every gift and every tribe is special to Him.

You need to know, that it doesn't matter if you are in a room where everyone has the same gift, you are unique and Adonai desires the gift you have to offer.

The gifts that the children of Israel gave to Adonai for the service of the Tabernacle, were things He had already given to them. Adonai has gifts for us as well to use for His service.

Through Yeshua, we receive the gift of salvation.
The gifts of the Ruach (Spirit). 1 Corinthians 12
The fruit of the Ruach (Spirit). Galatians 5:22-23
Gifts for serving in the ministry of Adonai. Romans 12:4-8, Ephesians 4:10-13

In the Book of James, chapter 1 verse 17, the apostle James tells us that, "Every good and perfect gift comes from the Father above."

What gift do you have to offer to Adonai for His Kingdom service?

PRACTICAL APPLICATIONS

DESIRING THE GIFTS FROM ADONAI!

Romans 12:6-8 MSG

"In this way we are like the various parts of a human body. Each part gets its meaning from the body as a whole, not the other way around. The body we're talking about is Christ's body of chosen people. Each of us finds our meaning and function as a part of his body. But as a chopped-off finger or cut-off toe we wouldn't amount to much, would we? So since we find ourselves fashioned into all these excellently formed and marvelously functioning parts in Christ's body, let's just go ahead and be what we were made to be, without enviously or pridefully comparing ourselves with each other, or trying to be something we aren't. If you preach, just preach God's Message, nothing else; if you help, just help, don't take over; if you teach, stick to your teaching; if you give encouraging guidance, be careful that you don't get bossy; if you're put in charge, don't manipulate; if you're called to give aid to people in distress, keep your eyes open and be quick to respond; if you work with the disadvantaged, don't let yourself get irritated with them or depressed by them. Keep a smile on your face."

FOR CHILDREN 4-6 YEARS OLD

Ask your parents to read Romans 12:4-8 for you. Then pray and ask the Ruach HaKodesh (Holy Spirit) to tell you which gift Adonai has given you to use for His service.

FOR CHILDREN 7-12 YEARS OLD

Read Romans 12:4-8, Pray, and ask the Ruach HaKodesh (Holy Spirit) to tell you which gift Adonai has given you to use for His service.

FOLLOW-UP FROM THE LAST TORAH PORTION

Ask who wants to share from last week's practical application

FOR CHILDREN 4-6 YEARS OLD

Practice being a good helper for your parents.

FOR CHILDREN 7-12 YEARS OLD

Pray and ask God to show you where you can be of help to someone. Also, if you need help with school, or having a difficult time with someone, ask God to send you the right people who can help you.

QUESTIONS - TEACHERS ANSWER KEY

1. **Who was in charge of the sons of Levi?**
   Ithamar

2. **Whose duty was it to count the sons of Gershon, Kohath, and Merari?**
   Moses, Aaron, the Tribal Leaders

3. **What was the age of the men counted to serve as priests to Aaron?**
   30-50 years

4. **Which of the sons of Levi is responsible for the curtains and covers of the Tabernacle?**
   Gershon

5. **Who was responsible for carrying the frames of the Tabernacle, its crossbars, posts, tent pegs, and ropes?**
   Merari

6. **What is the Jealousy Ritual called?**
   Sotah Trial

7. **What does it mean to be a Nazarite?** (Allow children to give answers according to their understanding.) Someone who desires to separate and consecrate his/herself to Adonai for a specific time.

8. **When Aaron and his sons bless the people what are they putting on them?**
   The Name of Adonai

9. **To whom were gifts from the leaders brought as offerings given?**
   The Levites

10. **What was the duty of the sons of Kohath?**
    To carry the holy items on their shoulders

QUESTIONS - CHILDREN'S COPY

1. Who was in charge of the sons of Levi?

2. Whose duty was it to count the sons of Gershon, Kohath, and Merari?

3. What was the age of the men counted to serve as priests to Aaron?

4. Which of the sons of Levi is responsible for the curtains and covers of the Tabernacle?

5. Who was responsible for carrying the frames of the Tabernacle, its crossbars, posts, tent pegs, and ropes?

6. What is the Jealousy Ritual called?

7. What does it mean to be a Nazarite?

8. When Aaron and his sons bless the people what are they putting on them?

9. To whom were the leaders brought as offerings given?

10. What was the duty of the sons of Kohath?

CRAFTS SUPPLIES FOR TORAH PORTION NASSO

SUPPLIES:
1. 12×12" Cardstock of Bright Color.
2. Print White Paper.
3. Glue Sticks.
4. Scissors.
5. Markers, Pencils, Crayons.
6. Gems.

CRAFTS:

1. Trace your hand on a folded piece of paper as a blessing sign. Make sure the thumb touches where the paper is folded.
2. Cut out the traced hand, except for the thumb part.

3. Paste the Aaronic blessing in Hebrew on the left hand.
4. Color and decorate the Aaronic blessing header and paste it on top of the cardstock.

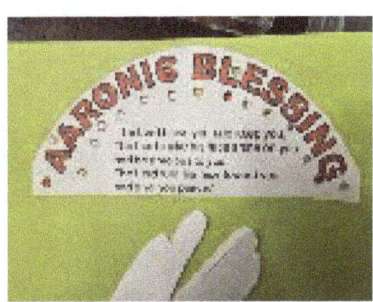

5. Color and decorate the flowers and paste 1 on each side.

6. Paste the hand, just one hand in the middle, so you can open them.

FINISHED ARTWORK

Beha'alotcha

"When You Set Up"

Torah Portion 36: Beha'alotcha "When You Set Up"

The Title of this week's Torah portion is **Beha'alotcha**. It is the Hebrew for the phrase ***"when you set up."*** It is found in the second verse of our Torah reading.

Numbers 8:1-2 AMP
Then the Lord spoke to Moses, saying, **2** "Speak to Aaron and say to him, '***When you set up*** and light the lamps, the seven lamps will shine in front of the lampstand.'"

Scripture Readings:
Numbers 8:1-12:16, Zechariah 2:10-4:7, Matthew 14:14-21, Psalm 68

The Theme of the Torah Portion:

Cloud and Fire

Theme Scripture:
Numbers 9:15 Amplified (AMP)

Now on the day that the tabernacle was erected, the cloud [of God's presence] covered the tabernacle, that is, the tent of the Testimony; and in the evening it was over the tabernacle, appearing like [a pillar of] fire until the morning.

Torah Portion Outline

- Lighting the Menorah, **Numbers 8:1-4**
- Consecrating the Levites, **Numbers 8:5-22**
- Training for the Levites, **Numbers 8:23-26**
- Passover Offerings, **Numbers 9:1-14**
- Fire and Cloud Journey, **Numbers 9:15-23**
- Silver Trumpets and its Purpose, **Numbers 10:1-9**
- The Traveling Order of the Camps, **Numbers 10:10-29**
- Moses' Invitation to His Father-in-law, **Numbers 10:30-33**
- First Journey of the Camps and the Ark, **Numbers 10:34-36**
- Fire of Adonai Blazed Against Complainers, **Numbers 11:2-3**
- Children of Israel Complain for Meat, **Numbers 11:4-10**
- Moses Cry for Help, **Numbers 11:11-15**
- The Appointment of the 70 Elders, **Numbers 11:16-17**
- Quail From the Sea, **Numbers 11:18-35**
- Miriam and Aaron Criticized Moses, **Numbers 12:1-9**
- Miriam Qurantied for Leprosy, **Numbers 12:10-16**

LESSON SUMMARY

In this week's Torah portion, Adonai gives Moses instructions for Aaron to light the Menorah. The Levites were consecrated and presented before Adonai as a wave offering by Aaron to begin their service in the Tabernacle. The Levites, aged twenty-five (25) years old and older, were to present themselves for service in the Tent of Meeting. At age fifty (50), they were to retire from their work and service in the Tabernacle. After the age of fifty (50), they were only to assist the younger brothers with their duties.

Adonai told Moses that they were to observe Passover at the appointed time. On the fourteenth day of the first month, they celebrated Passover. On the day of Passover, some of the men could not celebrate. The men went to Moses and Aaron and told them they were unable to celebrate Passover. They were defiled by a dead man's body. The men asked Moses, why it is that they shouldn't be allowed to present their offering to Adonai? Moses enquired of the Lord for instructions. Adonai appointed a second Passover. It was to be celebrated in the second month, on the fourteenth day. It was for anyone who was defiled, or who was traveling far away during the first month and could not observe Passover.

A cloud appeared like fire and rested over the Tabernacle the day it was set up. The cloud rested from evening until morning. This was a sign from Adonai to show the children of Israel when to pack up camp and travel. They knew it was time to travel whenever the cloud lifted from the Tabernacle. Wherever the cloud rested, they would set up camp. Whether the cloud rested for a few days, a week, a month, or a few hours, the children of Israel would set out to travel or remain camped by the word of Adonai. They traveled in order of their camps.

Orders were also given to make two silver trumpets, which were used to sound an alarm to gather the people. If both were sounded, the whole community would gather at the entrance of the Tent of Meeting.

The trumpets were also sounded at new moons, times of rejoicing, feasts, and over their burnt offerings and fellowship offerings. If only one trumpet was sounded, then the tribal leaders would gather towards Moses. The sound of the trumpets with a short blast was for the camps to set out and travel according to the order of their divisions. The camps from the east, led by the tribe of Judah, set out first. Then the Tabernacle was disassembled and carried out by the sons of Merari and Gershon. Next, the tribes in the south set out, led by the tribe of Reuben followed by the sons of Kothath carrying the Holy items. This allowed for the Tabernacle to be set up before the remainder of the tribes arrived. The camps from the west followed the sons of Kathath, led by the tribe of Ephraim. The last to set out were the camps from the north, led by the tribe of Dan, as the rear guard.

As they prepared for their first journey, Moses invited his father-in-law to travel with them. Instead, his father-in-law returned home to his own country and people. The Ark of the Covenant set out ahead of them for three days to find the resting place. The people were complaining, and Adonai heard their complaints. His anger burned, and Adonai set ablaze a fire at the edge of the camp which consumed the complainers. The people cried out to Moses, and he prayed to Adonai for the fire to cease. Adonai extinguished the fire. That place was called Tebareh because Adonai's fire burned among them.

The children of Israel complained again because they were not satisfied with the Mana they were eating. They wanted meat to eat. Moses became frustrated with the people. He cried out to Adonai for help. Adonai told Moses to gather the seventy (70) elders, the leaders from the twelve (12) tribes, and come before Him at the Tent of Meeting. Moses did as Adonai commanded. Adonai took some of the Ruach's (Spirit) anointing that was on Moses and anointed the seventy elders. Adonai appointed these leaders to help Moses with his responsibilities. They helped him carry the burden of the people. As for the people who were complaining about meat, Adonai caused a wind to carry quails in from the sea. The quails filled the camp and its surroundings. The people could walk a day's journey in any direction around the camp and find quails. The people went out and gathered the quails from night until morning. While they were eating, even before they swallowed the meat, the anger of the Lord broke out against them. He struck them with a severe plague. The place was called Kibroth-hattaavah because they buried the people who were craving meat.

Miriam and Aaron criticized Moses because of his wife. Adonai heard them speaking and was displeased with their behavior. He called Moses, Miriam, and Aaron to come and have a talk with Him in the Tent of Meeting. Adonai declared His displeasure with them for speaking against His servant Moses. Miriam was disciplined with Tza'arat (leprosy) for Lashon Hara. Aaron pleaded with Moses for mercy on behalf of Miriam, their sister. Moses cried to Adonai to heal her immediately, but Adonai said she must bear her shame. She had to remain outside the camp for seven days. The children of Israel remained in the camp and could not travel until Miriam was brought back into the camp. After Miriam was brought back into the camp, they left Hazeroth and camped in the wilderness of Paran.

LESSON DISCUSSION

FIRE TALK: A GUIDE OR JUDGEMENT

The children of Israel were now functioning as a community of people with rules and regulations for everyday life. The presence of Adonai guided them as a cloud by day and as fire by night.

Numbers 8:1— Then the Lord spoke to Moses, saying, **2** "Speak to Aaron and say to him, 'When you mount the lamps, the seven lamps will provide light in the front of the lampstand.'"

Numbers 9:15-17 — Now on the day that the tabernacle was erected, the cloud covered the tabernacle, the tent of the testimony, and in the evening it was like the appearance of fire over the tabernacle until morning. **16** That is how it was continuously; the cloud would cover it by day, and the appearance of fire by night. **17** Whenever the cloud was lifted from over the tent, afterward the sons of Israel would set out; and in the place where the cloud settled down, there the sons of Israel would camp.

The Mutterings and complaints of the children of Israel grieved Adonai. The fire of His presence which guided them became a consuming fire when they complained against Adonai. Moses and Miriam complained but they were not consumed because they did not murmur against Adonai.

1. They complained about hardships in the wilderness. **Numbers 11:1-3**

2. The mixed crowds (believed to be those who joined them from Egypt) and the children of Israel complained about having an easier life in Egypt and were craving meat to eat instead of Manna. **Numbers 11:4-9**

3. Moses complained to God because he felt as if he was the one carrying the burden of the people. **Numbers 11:10-16**

4. Miriam and Aaron criticized Moses because of his wife. **Numbers 12:1-2**

A Guide or a Consuming Fire?

No other nation had a god who was personally involved in the daily lives of the people. Yet, the children of Israel sometimes did not show appreciation for Adonai or His presence among them.

The fire of Adonai was a guide for the people, but it also consumed them in his anger because of their complaints. We too sometimes forget the goodness of God and behave as they did.

How are you experiencing the fire of Adonai? If the presence of Adonai shows up as fire in your life based on your actions, will He be a guide or a consuming fire?

God is a consuming fire. **Deuteronomy 4:24, Hebrews 12:28-29**
Grieve not the Holy Spirit (Ruach HaKodesh).

How do we grieve the Ruach HaKodesh? With our actions and words.

Ephesians 4: 29-32 MSG — Watch the way you talk. Let nothing foul or dirty come out of your mouth. Say only what helps, each word a gift. **30** Don't grieve God. Don't break his heart. His Holy Spirit, moving and breathing in you, is the most intimate part of your life, making you fit for Himself. Don't take such a gift for granted.
31-32 Make a clean break with all cutting, backbiting, profane talk. Be gentle with one another, sensitive. Forgive one another as quickly and thoroughly as God in Christ forgave you.

TURNING POINT:

SILVER TRUMPETS: TO HEAR AND KNOW

Numbers 10:1-10 NASB

The Lord spoke further to Moses, saying, **2** "Make yourself two trumpets of silver, you shall make them of hammered work; and you shall use them for summoning the congregation and breaking camp. **3** Now when both are blown, all the congregation shall meet you at the entrance of the tent of meeting. **4** But if only one is blown, then the leaders, the heads of the divisions of Israel, shall meet you. **5** And when you blow an alarm, the camps that are pitched on the east side shall set out. **6** Then when you sound an alarm the second time, the camps that are pitched on the south side shall set out; an alarm is to be sounded for them to break camp. **7** When convening the assembly, however, you shall blow the trumpets without sounding an alarm. **8** The sons of Aaron, moreover, the priests, shall blow the trumpets; and this shall be a permanent statute for you throughout your generations. **9** And when you go to war in your land against the enemy who attacks you, then you shall sound an alarm with the trumpets, so that you will be thought of by the Lord your God, and be saved from your enemies. **10** Also on the day of your joy and at your appointed [al]feasts, and on the first days of your months, you shall blow the trumpets over your burnt offerings, and over the sacrifices of your peace offerings; and they shall be as a reminder of you before your God. I am the Lord your God."

Adonai gave Moses instructions to make two silver trumpets. They were used to gather the people and used when the people were to pull down the Tabernacle and move on. There were distinct sounds used for the gathering of the people to Adonai, for gathering the leaders to Moses, and for gathering all the children of Israel to Moses. There was a different sound for war. There were also specific times when either both or one trumpet was blown to sound an alarm. Moses had to teach the people not only to hear the sounds but also to know the purpose of the different sounds so there would not be any confusion in the camp.

Have you ever experienced a fire drill at school? A teacher usually announces when there will be a fire drill. This is done so you will know what to do when there is a fire or an emergency on campus. When you hear the sounds, you know the purpose. There will come a day when Adonai will sound a trumpet to gather His people together to Himself. Only those who hear and know the purpose of the sound will gather before Him.

1 Thessalonians 4:16-17 NASB — For the Lord Himself will descend from heaven with a shout, with the voice of the archangel and with the trumpet of God, and the dead in Christ will rise first. **17** Then we who are alive, who remain, will be caught up together with them in the clouds to meet the Lord in the air, and so we will always be with the Lord.

How do you prepare to hear the trumpet of Adonai?
Yeshua said; when you hear the words of Adonai and obey them, we are practicing hearing the sound.

"My sheep knows my voice and they follow me" **John 10:27**. The voice of Yeshua, is the word of Adonai.

The Ruach also speaks to us **(Read 2 Timothy 3:14-17)**. When we hear and obey Him, we practice hearing and knowing the purpose of the sound of the trumpet.

PRACTICAL APPLICATIONS

FOR CHILDREN 4-6 YEARS OLD
Practice being thankful to your parents instead of complaining when you don't get your way.

FOR CHILDREN 7-12 YEARS OLD
Be aware of your actions and attitude. Don't be a complainer! Practice being thankful, even when you think you have the right to complain.

FOLLOW-UP FROM THE LAST TORAH PORTION
Ask who wants to share from last week's practical application.

FOR CHILDREN 4-6 YEARS OLD
Ask your parents to read Romans 12:4-8 for you. Then pray and ask the Ruach HaKodesh (Holy Spirit) to tell you which gift Adonai has given you to use for His service.

FOR CHILDREN 7-12 YEARS OLD
Read Romans 12:4-8, Pray, and ask the Ruach HaKodesh (Holy Spirit) to tell you which gift Adonai has given you to use for His service.

QUESTIONS - TEACHERS ANSWER KEY

1. **Who was in charge of lighting the Menorah?**
   Aaron

2. **At what age did the Levites begin their training?**
   25

3. **When the Levites were consecrated, they were presented to Adonai and _____ as an offering to Him.**
   Waved

4. **How did the presence of Adonai appear above the Tabernacle?**
   Cloud by day and fire by night

5. **How many elders were anointed to help Moses?**
   70

6. **How were they anointed?**
   Adonai took from the anointing of the Ruach that was on Moses and put it on them

7. What was one of the purposes of the silver trumpets?
   To assemble the children of Israel or to disassemble the camp to move

8. **What did the people get when they cried for meat?**
   Quail

9. **On what special days were the trumpets sound?**
   New moons, feast days, times of rejoicing

10. **For what reason was Miriam afflicted with Tza'arat (leprosy)?**
    For criticizing Moses

QUESTIONS - CHILDREN'S COPY

1. Who was in charge of lighting the Menorah?

2. At what age did the Levites begin their training?

3. When the Levites were consecrated, they were presented to Adonai and _____ as an offering to Him.

4. How did the presence of Adonai appear above the Tabernacle?

5. How many elders were anointed to help Moses?

6. How were they anointed?

7. What was one of the purposes of the silver trumpets?

8. What did the people get when they cried for meat?

9. On what special days were the trumpets sound?

10. For what reason was Miriam afflicted with Tza'arat (leprosy)?

CRAFTS FOR TORAH PORTION BEHA'ALOTCHA

SUPPLIES:
1. 12x12" Black Cardstock
2. 12×12" Blue Cardstock
3. Print Paper
4. Red Construction Paper
5. Orange Construction Paper
6. Yellow Construction Paper
7. Cotton Balls
8. Star Stickers
9. Sequins
10. Markers, Pencils
11. Glue and Glue Sticks

CRAFTS:

1. Children will receive a prepared folder made out of black and blue cardstock taped together
2. They will receive TWO pre-cut drawings of the Tent of the Meeting

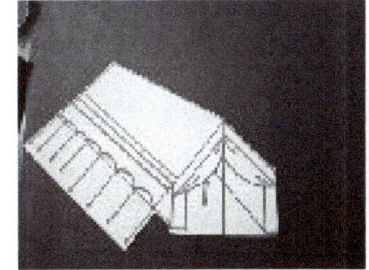 

3. Color the Tent of Meeting
4. Glue one on the black side and one on the blue
5. On the black side, put star stickers to indicate a starry night

6. On the right side, glue precut fire flames. Red first, then orange, then yellow

7. On the blue side, glue cotton balls to indicate the pillar of cloud
8. Glue sequins coming out from the cloud

9. Color the headers of Fire by Night and Pillar of Cloud

10. Glue them on the bottom

Shelach Lecha

"Send on Your Behalf"

Torah Portion 37: Shelach Lecha "Send on Your Behalf"

The title of this week's Torah Portion is **Shelach Lecha** which is translated as ***"send on your behalf."*** It is found in the second verse of our Torah reading.

Numbers 13:2 CJB

"***Send*** some men on ***your behalf*** to investigate the land of Canaan, which I am giving to Bnei-Yisrael. Each man you are to send will be a prince of the tribe of his fathers, a man from each tribe."

Scripture Readings:
Numbers 13:1-15:41, Joshua 2:1-24, Matthew 10:1-14, Psalm 64

The Theme of the Torah Portion:

Where is your faith?

Scripture for Theme

Numbers 14:11 Artscroll Translation

Hashem said to Moses, "How long will this people provoke Me, and how long will they not have faith in Me, despite all the signs that I have performed in their midst?"

Torah Portion Outline

- Sending Out the Spies, **Numbers 13:1-24**
- The Report of the 10 Spies, **Numbers 13:25-29**
- Caleb's Report, **Numbers 13:30-33**
- The People Rebel against God's Command, **Numbers 14:1-4**
- Joshua & Caleb Encourage the People, **Numbers 14:5-10**
- Moses Prays for the People, **Numbers 14:11-29**
- Adonai Forgives the People for Their Rebellion, **Numbers 14:20-26**
- Israel is Punished for Their Rebellion Against God, **Numbers 14:27-5**
- Laws for When Israel Enters Canaan, **Numbers 15:1-13**
- Laws for Strangers Who Join Israel, **Numbers 15:14-16**
- Laws for Grain Offerings in the Land, **Numbers 15:17-21**
- Laws Regarding Public and Individual Idol Worship, **Numbers 15:22-31**
- Punishment for Breaking the Sabbath, **Numbers 15:32-36**
- Command to Make Zitzit, **Numbers 15:37-41**

LESSON SUMMARY

Last week's Torah portion ended with Miriam's return to the camp and the children of Israel traveling from Hazeroth and camping in the wilderness of Paran. Adonai had commanded them by the mouth of Moses to go and possess the land of Canaan that He had promised to Abraham. We learn in this week's Torah portion that Moses sent some men to spy out the promised land. He sent twelve men, who were leaders and princes from each tribe. Among the twelve leaders were Hoshea, the son of Nun from the tribe of Ephraim, whom Moses called Joshua, and Caleb the son of Jephunneh, from the tribe of Judah. Moses told the twelve men to explore the land from the city of Negev to the hill country of Hebron. He also told them to be courageous and bring back some of the fruits from the land. The spies went into the land according to Moses' command. For forty (40) days, they went throughout the land from the wilderness of Paran to Hebron.

After their return, the spies brought their report to Moses, Aaron, and the congregation of Israel. They also brought back pomegranates, figs, and a cluster of grapes they cut in the Eschol Valley. The cluster was too large for one person to carry. They had to put it on a stick for two men to carry on their shoulders. The spies gave a bad report to Moses about the land, except for Caleb and Joshua. They reported to Moses that the land flows with milk and honey, as Adonai had promised. They reported that the people living in the land were powerful, the cities were very large, and the cities were fortified. Caleb tried to encourage the people, but the men who went up with him discouraged the people's hearts, saying, We cannot attack these people because they are stronger than us; they will devour us and take our wives and children captives. All the men we saw were giants. We seemed like grasshoppers in our eyes as well as theirs. The people were sorely discouraged. They cried all night with loud voices. They grumbled against Moses and Aaron. The children of Israel even said that it was because God did not love them that He brought them out of Egypt for them to die by the sword. They thought it would be better for them to return to Egypt. They said to each other, Let's choose a leader and return to Egypt.

Moses and Aaron fell on their faces before the congregation of Israel. Joshua and Caleb tore their clothes, cried out to the people, and said to them, "Don't rebel against Adonai. The land is very good; if Adonai is pleased with us, He will lead us and give us the land. Don't be afraid of the people in the land; Adonai is with us." The Lord was angry with the people. He wanted to strike them with a plague and destroy them all. God told Moses He would kill them all and instead make him a great nation, however, Moses appealed to the mercy of Adonai and asked Him to forgive the people. Don't destroy them all at once, because the Egyptians will hear about it. Adonai listened to Moses and forgave the people, but He swore only Caleb, Joshua, and their descendants would inherit the land He promised them. They would suffer the punishment for their guilt. Forty years, one year for each day they spent in the land because they rebelled against My word. You will die in the wilderness. Your sons, whom you say will become captives, will be shepherds in the wilderness and suffer punishment for your unfaithfulness. The ten men who brought back a bad report were killed by a plague from Adonai. The next morning, the children of Israel disobeyed the word of Adonai once more in an attempt to go and possess the land, but the Lord was not with them. Neither Moses nor the Ark of Adonai's covenant were with them. The Amalekites and Canaanites living in the mountain country came down, attacked, and defeated them.

Adonai spoke to Moses again and gave him instructions for the offering the children of Israel were to present to Him when they entered the land and made their homes. He also commanded that the rules and commandments He has given for the children of Israel are the same for any outsider who wants to join the community of Israel. Additional instruction was given for anyone who intentionally failed to keep the commandments of Adonai and also for those if the whole community sinned by publicly worshiping idols or an individual. The commandment to make tzitzit on their garments was given to the children of Israel so they would look upon them and remember all the commands of Adonai. To do them and be holy, so they would not go after the desires of their hearts and eyes. The Torah portion ends with Adonai reminding the children of Israel three times that He is Adonai, their God, who brought them out of Egypt.

LESSON DISCUSSION

WHOSE REPORT WILL YOU BELIEVE?

From last week's Torah portion, we see a pattern of negative behavior among the children of Israel. They complained and murmured against God and his servants, Moses and Aaron. Even Moses was affected by their negative behavior when he petitioned God for help. In this week's Torah portion, Moses sent out twelve spies to search out the land of Canaan. Ten of the spies came back with an evil report and turned the hearts of the people against Adonai, but two remained faithful, trusting in the words of Adonai.

Numbers 13:25-32 NASB
When they returned from spying out the land, at the end of forty days, **26** they proceeded to come to Moses and Aaron and to all the congregation of the sons of Israel in the wilderness of Paran, at Kadesh; and they brought back word to them and to all the congregation and showed them the fruit of the land. **27** Thus they told him, and said, "We went in to the land where you sent us; and it certainly does flow with milk and honey, and this is its fruit.
28 Nevertheless, the people who live in the land are strong, and the cities are fortified and very large; and moreover, we saw the descendants of Anak there. **29** Amalek is living in the land of the Negev and the Hittites and the Jebusites and the Amorites are living in the hill country, and the Canaanites are living by the sea and by the side of the Jordan." **30** Then Caleb quieted the people before Moses and said, "We should by all means go up and take possession of it, for we will surely overcome it." **31** But the men who had gone up with him said, "We are not able to go up against the people, for they are too strong for us." **32** So they gave out to the sons of Israel a bad report of the land which they had spied out, saying, "The land through which we have gone, in spying it out, is a land that devours its inhabitants; and all the people whom we saw in it are men of great size. **33** There also we saw the Nephilim (the sons of Anak are part of the Nephilim);

and we became like grasshoppers in our own sight, and so we were in their sight."

Negatives Attributes (qualities) of the Children of Israel:
- They Were Fearful
- They Lacked faith
- They Were Rebellious
- They Provoked Adonai to Anger

Among all the spies, only Caleb and Joshua believed the word of Adonai and were ready to possess the land. They tried to encourage the people to obey the words of Adonai, but the people rebelled and wanted to ston them instead.

Numbers 16:6-10 NASB

Joshua the son of Nun and Caleb the son of Jephunneh, of those who had spied out the land, tore their clothes; **7** and they spoke to all the congregation of the sons of Israel, saying, "The land which we passed through to spy out is an exceedingly good land. **8** If the Lord is pleased with us, then He will bring us into this land and give it to us—a land which flows with milk and honey. **9** Only do not rebel against the Lord; and do not fear the people of the land, for they will be our prey. Their protection has been removed from them, and the Lord is with us; do not fear them." **10** But all the congregation said to stone them with stones. Then the glory of the Lord appeared in the tent of meeting to all the sons of Israel.

Positive Attributes (qualities) of Caleb and Joshua:
- They Trusted and Obeyed
- They Believed That With God They Would Possess the Land
- They Were Courageous and had Confidence in Adonai's Power to Protect Them and Deliver Them From the Enemy
- They Were Faithful and Encouraging to Their Brothers and Sisters

Trust and Obey

Our obedience to the Word of God demonstrates our trust in Him. When we don't obey His voice or commandments, we do not trust Him. When we refuse to obey those whom He has given the authority to protect us and care for us, such as our parents, teachers, pastors, and other guardians, then we rebel against God, just like the children of Israel did with Moses and Aaron.

Hebrews 3:12-14 MSG (The Message Bible)
12-14 So watch your step, friends. Make sure there's no evil unbelief lying around that will trip you up and throw you off course, diverting you from the living God. For as long as God's still calling it Today, keep each other on your toes so sin doesn't slow down your reflexes. If we can only keep our grip on the sure thing we started out with, we're in this with Christ for the long haul. These words keep ringing in our ears: Today, please listen; don't turn a deaf ear as in the bitter uprising.

It is not always easy to obey because doing what is right is not usually what is popular. We can learn to demonstrate obedience and trust in Adonai when we do what is right, even when it is hard.

Yeshua demonstrated obedience and trust in the Father so we can turn to Him for help.

Hebrew 5:8 MSG
Though he was God's Son, he learned trusting-obedience by what he suffered, just as we do. Then, having arrived at the full stature of his maturity and having been announced by God as high priest in the order of Melchizedek, he became the source of eternal salvation to all who believingly obey him.

Be aware of the attributes of your friends. Bad company will lead you away from the word of God.

Be aware of your attributes. Are you leading your friends towards or away from Adonai?

TURNING POINT:

YESHUA: MY TZITZIT A TANGLE REMINDER

The children of Israel's eyes and hearts were fixed on the wrong things and the wrong places when they went to spy out the land of Canaan. Instead of keeping their focus on the good things of the land that Adonai had given them; they became consumed with the giants they saw, and their hearts became fearful. They forgot all the miracles and signs Adonai had performed in Egypt along with His provision and protection in the wilderness. Their wandering hearts and eyes led them down a path of rebellion. To help them, Adonai gave Moses instructions for the children of Israel to make Tzitzit and attach them to the four corners of their clothes. The Tzitzit was for the children of Israel to look at and remember all the commandments of Adonai. It was a physical reminder for them to do all God's commandments and to not follow after their own hearts and eyes, and by doing so, not to go astray. The Tzitzit was also a reminder to be holy because Adonai, their God who brought them out of Egypt, is holy (Numbers 15:37-41).

The Tzitzit was a physical reminder of the commandments of Adonai. Traditionally, only men wear Tzitzit, but as children of God, we are all commanded to keep His commandments. Likewise, Yeshua's death and resurrection are reminders to us that we belong to Adonai if we put our trust in Him. When we keep our hearts and eyes fixed on Yeshua, we will be reminded to obey our Heavenly Father's commands and be holy, for He is holy.

Keep your eye and heart on Yeshua!

PRACTICAL APPLICATIONS
BRINGING GOOD NEWS

FOR CHILDREN 4-6 YEARS OLD
Choose one of the qualities of Joshua and Caleb and demonstrate it this week.

FOR CHILDREN 7-12 YEARS OLD
Choose one of the qualities from Joshua and Caleb and demonstrate it this week.

Practice to only speak good things. Share something good God has done for you with a family member or friend.

FOLLOW-UP FROM THE LAST TORAH PORTION
Ask who wants to share from last week's practical application.

FOR CHILDREN 4-6 YEARS OLD
Practice being thankful to your parents instead of complaining when you don't get your way.

FOR CHILDREN 7-12 YEARS OLD
Be aware of your actions and attitude. Don't be a complainer! Practice being thankful, even when you think you have the right to complain.

QUESTIONS - TEACHERS ANSWER KEY

1. **What is the name of the place where the spies cut grapes?**
   The Valley of Eshcol

2. **How many spies were sent into the land?**
   Twelve (12)

3. **After how many days did the spies return?**
   Forty (40) days

4. **What was Joshua's birth name?**
   Hoshea

5. **The giants in the land were whose descendants?**
   Anak

6. **How many years were the children of Israel punished for their rebellion?**

7. **Forty (40) years**

8. **How many times did Adonai say the children of Israel tested Him?**
   Ten (10) times (Numbers 14:22)

9. **Name two other nations that lived in the land they went to spy out.**
   Amalekites, Hittites, Jebusites, Amorites, and Canaanites

10. **How many men did it take to carry the cluster of grapes?**
    Two (2) men

11. **What other fruits did they bring back from the land?**
    Pomegranates and figs

12. **Which were the only two men of the twelve spies who would enter the promised land?**
    Caleb and Joshua

QUESTIONS - CHILDREN'S COPY

1. What is the name of the place where the spies cut grapes?

2. How many spies were sent into the land?

3. After how many days did the spies return?

4. What was Joshua's birth name?

5. The giants in the land were whose descendants?

6. How many years were the children of Israel punished for their rebellion?

7. How many times did Adonai say the children of Israel tested Him?

8. Name two other nations that lived in the land they went to spy out.

9. How many men did it take to carry the cluster of grapes?

10. What other fruits did they bring back from the land?

11. Which were the only two men of the twelve spies who would enter the promised land?

CRAFTS SUPPLIES FOR TORAH PORTION SHELACH

SUPPLIES:
1. Pink Construction Paper
2. White Print Paper
3. Purple Cardstock Paper
4. Blue Construction Paper
5. Green Construction Paper
6. Glue Sticks
7. Coloring Supplies
8. Pen or Pencil

CRAFTS: Fruit of Obedience

1. Children will receive pink construction paper folded as shown.
2. They will paste 3 green leaves on top as shown and draw leaf veins on top.
3. They will receive pre-cut blue and purple circles for grapes.

4. Children will start pasting them:
    a) Alternate blue and purple.
    b) Overlap rows so it looks like grapes.
5. Draw a stem.
6. Along the stem, write: why were they different?
7. Write the qualities of Caleb and Joshua that made them different from the other 10 spies.

8. Color words "Caleb, Joshua, Trust, Obey." (Drawn by graffiti artist Joel Calendrillo.)

9. Paste them as shown, on the inside and outside of the pamphlet.

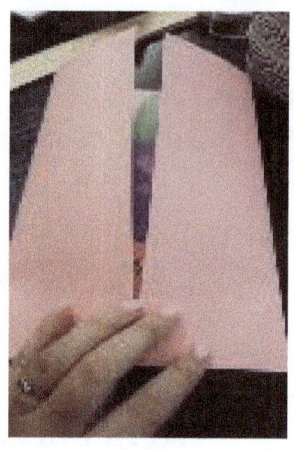

FINISHED ARTWORK

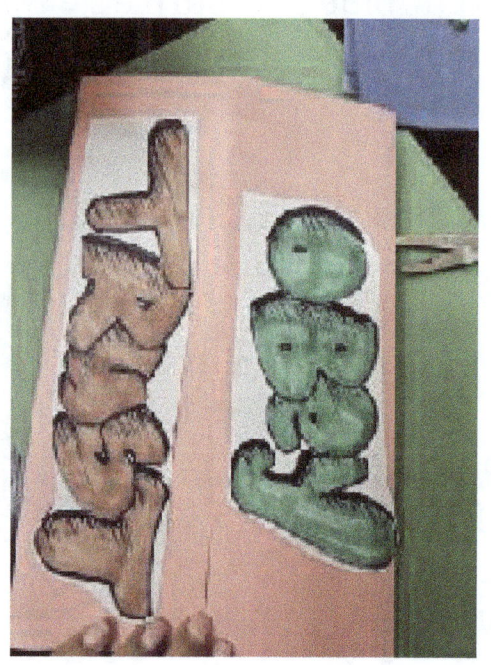

Korach

"Bald"

Torah Portion 38: Korach "Korah"

The title of this week's Torah Portion is **Korach** (Korah) which means *"**bald.**"* Korach is the name of the Levite who started a rebellion against Moses in this Torah Portion reading. His name means "bald" or "make oneself bald". Although the meaning of his name is not mentioned in the Torah reading, it is implied because of the death of all those who joined in his rebellion, while the others mourned. It was the custom to shave one's head when they are mourning the death of someone.

Numbers 16:1-2 NASB
Now Korah the son of Izhar, the son of Kohath, the son of Levi, with Dathan and Abiram, the sons of Eliab, and On the son of Peleth, sons of Reuben, took action, **2** and they rose up before Moses, together with some of the sons of Israel, two hundred and fifty leaders of the congregation, chosen in the assembly, men of renown.

Scripture Readings:
Numbers 16:1-18:32, 1Samuel 11:14-12:22, Matthew 26:13-24, Psalm 5

The Theme of the Torah Portion:
Putting a Stop to Israel's Complaints

Scripture for Theme

Numbers 17:5 WEB (World English Bible)
It shall happen that the rod of the man whom I shall choose shall bud. I will make the murmurings of the children of Israel, which they murmur against you, cease from me."

Torah Portion Outline

- Korach Rebellion, **Numbers 16:1-7**
- Moses Response to Korach, **Numbers 16:8-19**
- God's Response to Korach, **Numbers 16:20-30**
- Punishment for Korach's Rebellion, **Numbers 16:31-40**
- Moses and Aaron Accused of Murder, **Numbers 16:41-50**
- Aaron's Rod Blooms, **Numbers 17:1-13**
- Duties for Aaron and the Levites Reaffirmed, **Numbers 18:1-7**
- Offerings for the Priest, **Numbers 18:8-20**
- Tithes for the Levites, **Numbers 18:21-32**

LESSON SUMMARY

In last week's Torah portion, we learned about the twelve spies Moses sent to investigate the land of Canaan. Ten of the spies returned with a bad report that discouraged the people's hearts and prevented them from entering the land Adonai promised to give them. Only Joshua and Caleb remained faithful, believing that Adonai was able to give them the land as their possession. Adonai destroyed the ten spies who brought back a bad report. Adonai punished the children of Israel because they believed in the report of the spies instead of Him. They would wander in the wilderness for 40 years until that generation died. Only the children under twenty years of age, along with Joshua and Caleb, would live to enter the promised land. The Torah portion ended with Adonai's command to the children of Israel to make tzitzit and to attach them to the four corners of their garments. This was a sign, and a reminder to them, to keep all the commandments of Adonai.

In this week's Torah portion, Korah, the son of Izhar, a son of Levi, along with Dathan and Abiram, descendants of Reuben, gathered 250 men who were leaders in Israel, and turned against Moses by challenging his authority. They accused Moses of making himself more important than the rest of the people. They said to him, "All the people are holy, and the Lord is with them; you have gone too far." Moses told Korah that Adonai had chosen him and his brothers to help Aaron and his sons. Moses asked Korah, "Do you also want to be the priest?" Moses let Korah know he was rebelling against Adonai. Dothan and Abiram weren't with Korah at the time, so Moses sent a message to them to meet him, but they refused. Instead, they hurled insults at him, saying, "Isn't it enough that you have brought us from a land flowing with milk and honey to kill us in the wilderness?" "Would you also take from them all they have left?" Moses became angry at their words and said to Adonai, "I have not taken a donkey; I have not wronged one of them. Adonai destroyed Korah and his followers. He said to all the men, Take your censers, put fire and incense in them, and present them before Adonai. Adonai will come near to choose and show who is His, and who is holy. They did as Moses said and came to the entrance of the Tent of Meeting. The glory of Adonai appeared. Adonai wanted to destroy them all at once, but Moses pleaded for the innocent people. Adonai caused the earth to open up and swallow them. The fire of Adonai consumed the 250 leaders who also rebelled against Moses.

The next morning, the children of Israel grumbled against Moses and Aaron and accused them of "killing Adonai's people." Adonai's anger was great toward the people. He sent a plague into the camp, killing 14,700 people. Aaron didn't make atonement for the people for the plague to stop. Dissatisfied with the grumblings of the children of Israel about who is Adonai's chosen priest, Adonai told Moses to have the twelve leaders from each tribe take their rods and write their names on their rod, then place the rods in the Tent of Meeting before the Tent of Testimony. Aaron's name was to be written on his rod representing the tribe of Levi. The men gave Moses their rods as Adonai had commanded, and he placed them before the ark of the Testimony. The next morning, Moses entered the Tent of Testimony, and Aaron's rod from the tribe of Levi had sprouted, blossomed, and produced almonds. Moses brought the rods to the children of Israel. Each man took his rod, but Aaron's rod was put back in front of the Testimony to keep as a sign to the sons of rebellion, to put an end to their grumblings against Adonai, so they would not die.

The Torah reading concludes by reiterating the duties of the priesthood and their portions as an inheritance. Aaron and his sons were given charge of the Sanctuary and the duties of the priesthood. The Levites were chosen to help Aaron and his sons before the Tent of the Testimony, however, they could not approach the Sanctuary or the altar; doing so would cause their own deaths and the deaths of Aaron and his sons. Aaron and his sons were to receive whatever was set aside from the holy offerings that were presented to Adonai by the children of Israel. It was their permanent share. The Levites were not given any land as their inheritance. All the tithes given to Adonai belonged to them. Adonai was their inheritance. Adonai also commanded that when the Levites received the tithes that were given to them, they were to offer a tithe to Adonia from that tithe, which was then given to Aaron the priest. The Levites were to present the best and holiest part of their portion as an offering to Adonai, so they would not defile the holy things of the children of Israel and die.

LESSON DISCUSSION

WHOM WILL ADONAI CHOOSE?

In this Torah portion, Korah and his followers spoke badly about Moses:

"He made himself ruler over us…"
Numbers 16:1-3

Now Korah the son of Izhar, the son of Kohath, the son of Levi, with Dathan and Abiram, the sons of Eliab, and On the son of Peleth, sons of Reuben, took action, **2** and they rose up before Moses, together with some of the sons of Israel, two hundred and fifty leaders of the congregation, chosen in the assembly, men of renown. **3** They assembled together against Moses and Aaron, and said to them, *"You have gone far enough, for all the congregation are holy, every one of them, and the Lord is in their midst; so why do you exalt yourselves above the assembly of the Lord?"*

"Accused of being a thief…"
Numbers 16:13-15

Then Moses sent a summons to Dathan and Abiram, the sons of Eliab; but they said, "We will not come up. **13** Is it not enough that you have brought us up out of a land flowing with milk and honey to have us die in the wilderness, but you would also lord it over us? **14** Indeed, you have not brought us into a land flowing with milk and honey, nor have you given us an inheritance of fields and vineyards. Would you put out the eyes of these men? We will not come up!" **15** Then Moses became very angry and said to the Lord, "Do not regard their offering! *I have not taken a single donkey from them, nor have I done harm to any of them.*"

"Accused of murder…"
Numbers 16: 41

But on the next day all the congregation of the sons of Israel grumbled against Moses and Aaron, saying, "You are the ones who have caused the death of the Lord's people."

Although Moses was angry because of what the people were saying, he remained humble before Adonai. He did not allow himself to speak to them according to how he felt. He told them "Adonai will show", "Adonai will choose", and "Adonai will judge." Moses was confident, knowing that Adonai chose him as the leader and that Adonai would judge the people for their actions. Moses allowed Adonai to prove to the people that he and Aaron were chosen and appointed by Adonai. Adonai chose, He judged, and He showed them who was his. He caused the earth to split open and swallow up Korah, Dothan, Abiram, and their families. The 250 leaders were consumed by fire. A plague killed 14,700 of those who accused Moses and Aaron of causing their deaths. Moses and Aaron prayed for Adonai to have mercy on the people so the plague would stop. "Then Moses said to Aaron, "Take the censer, put into it fire from the altar and put in incense. Get going and hurry to the assembly and make atonement for them, because wrath has come out from Adonai and the plague has started." Aaron did just as Moses had said and ran into the middle of the assembly. Behold, the plague had already started among the people. But he offered the incense and made atonement for the people. He stood between the dead and the living and the plague stopped." **Numbers 16:46-48 TLV**

AARON IS THE MAN: A SIGN TO ALL, AN END TO THE GRUMBLINGS AGAINST ADONAI

Adonai not only judged the rebellious, but also reestablished the authority of Aaron as his chosen servant to lead the priesthood. All the leaders of the tribes were told to bring their staffs(rods) and write their names on them, place them before the Testimony in the Tent of Meeting, so that Adonai could cause the rod to sprout of the one He chose. Aaron's name was written on the staff belonging to the tribe of Levi.

Numbers 17:8-11
Now on the next day Moses went into the tent of the testimony; and behold, the rod of Aaron for the house of Levi had sprouted and put forth buds and produced blossoms, and it bore ripe almonds. **9** Moses then brought out all the rods from the presence of the Lord to all the sons of Israel; and they looked, and each man took his rod. **10** But the Lord said to Moses, "Put back the rod of Aaron before the testimony [af]to be kept as a sign against the rebels, that you may put an end to their grumblings against Me, so that they will not die." **11** Thus Moses did; just as the Lord had commanded him, so he did.

NOT MY WILL BUT YOURS ADONAI

In every situation, Moses bowed his face, in an act of prayer, asking for Adoani to have mercy on the people (Numbers 16:4, 22, 45,). How easy it would have been for Moses to allow Adonai to destroy all the people and make himself a great nation. Moses wanted only the best for the people and not only for himself.

Yeshua, while He was on earth also wanted what was best for all mankind. Even though surrendering His life was painful, He prayed for the will of the Father to be done.
Before He was arrested He could have saved Himself instead of dying for us. He could have called for twelve legions of angels to save Him, but instead, He said to the men who came for Him, **"Do what you came to do"** Matthew 26:47-54)

Moses and Yeshua laid down their life so the will of God could be accomplished through them. Yeshua said anyone who desires to follow

Him must give up the way he/she desires to live and to live the way the Father wants them to live. Matthew 16:24

Are you willing to live in obedience to the Torah so God's plan and purpose can be accomplished through you?

1 John 2:15-17 MSG

Don't love the world's ways. Don't love the world's goods. Love of the world squeezes out love for the Father. Practically everything that goes on in the world—wanting your own way, wanting everything for yourself, wanting to appear important—has nothing to do with the Father. It just isolates you from him. The world and all its wanting, wanting, wanting is on the way out—but whoever does what God wants is set for eternity.

TURNING POINT:

A SPECIAL INHERITANCE: ADONAI IS MY PORTION AND INHERITANCE

Numbers 18:19-21
All the offerings of the holy gifts, which the sons of Israel offer to the Lord, I have given to you and your sons and your daughters with you, as a perpetual allotment. It is an everlasting covenant of salt before the Lord to you and your descendants with you." **20 Then the Lord said to Aaron, "You shall have no inheritance in their land nor own any portion among them; I am your portion and your inheritance among the sons of Israel. 21** "To the sons of Levi, behold, I have given all the tithe in Israel for an inheritance, in return for their service which they perform, the service of the tent of meeting.

Can you imagine your parents giving all your siblings or friends gifts and not giving you anything? How would you feel?

All the children of Israel were promised land as their inheritance, except for Aaron and the Levites. How could this be? Doesn't Adonai want them to have something to call their own? The Levites were chosen as Adonai's firstborn, and as the firstborn, they were given what belonged to the father. Everything that was given to Adonai by the children of Israel was given to Aaron the priest and the Levites.

Psalm 24:1 tells us the earth belongs to the Lord and everything in it. The Levites received more than land in Israel as their inheritance, they received everything that belonged to Adonai.

Adonai said, "He is their portion and inheritance." As ministers of Adonai, they were attached to Him and not to the physical land given to Israel. This teaches us that no matter where they are, they belong to Him, and all He has belonged to them.

When you are chosen by Adonai, you are given the best. There is nothing greater than Adonai. To have Him as your inheritance means you have everything you need.

Adonai has chosen you and given you an inheritance through Yeshua. "Since we are his children, we are his heirs. In fact, together with Christ we are heirs of God's glory" (Romans 8:17)

2 Peter 3-4 (NLT)

By his divine power, God has given us everything we need for living a godly life. We have received all of this by coming to know him, the one who called us to himself by means of his marvelous glory and excellence. **4** And because of his glory and excellence, he has given us great and precious promises. These are the promises that enable you to share his divine nature and escape the world's corruption caused by human desires.

Don't forget your inheritance. Adonai is yours!!

PRACTICAL APPLICATIONS
LOVE LIKE MOSES

FOR CHILDREN 4-6 YEARS OLD
When someone makes you feel angry or hurt, talk to your parents about it and let them help you do the right thing about it.

FOR CHILDREN 7-12 YEARS OLD
When others speak badly about you, ask the Holy Spirit to help you respond in love knowing you are Adonai's son/daughter, and you were chosen to lead by example not to follow the crowd.

FOLLOW-UP FROM THE LAST TORAH PORTION
Ask who wants to share from last week's practical application.

PRACTICAL APPLICATIONS
BRINGING GOOD NEWS

FOR CHILDREN 4-6 YEARS OLD
Choose one of the qualities of Joshua and Caleb and demonstrate it this week.

FOR CHILDREN 7-12 YEARS OLD
Choose one of the qualities from Joshua and Caleb and demonstrate it this week.

Practice to only speak good things. Share something good God has done for you with a family member or friend.

QUESTIONS - TEACHERS ANSWER KEY

1. **Who started the rebellion against Moses?**
   Korah

2. **Name three of the men who were sons of the tribe of Reuben.**
   Dathan, Abiram, On

3. **How many leaders joined in the rebellion?**
   250

4. **How did Korah and the rebellious people die?**
   The earth swallowed them. 250 men burned with fire

5. **What did Aaron do to make atonement for the people?**
   He put fire and incense in his censer and offered atonement

6. **What was the cause of the plague that killed 14,700 people in the camp?**
   The people grumbled and accused Moses of "killing the People of God"

7. **Whom did Adonai choose as His priest?**
   Aaron

8. **What happened to Aaron's rod in the presence of Adonai?**
   It sprouted, blossomed, and produced almonds

9. **Who refused to come to Moses when they were called?**
   Dathan and Abiram

10. **What did the priests and the Levites receive as their inheritance instead of Land?**
    Adonai is their inheritance

QUESTIONS - CHILDREN'S COPY

1. Who started the rebellion against Moses?

2. Name three of the men who were sons of the tribe of Reuben.

3. How many leaders joined in the rebellion?

4. How did Korah and the rebellious people die?

5. What did Aaron do to make atonement for the people?

6. What was the cause of the plague that killed 14,700 people in the camp?

7. Whom did Adonai choose as His priest?

8. What happened to Aaron's rod in the presence of Adonai?

9. Who refused to come to Moses when they were called?

10. What did the priests and the Levites receive as their inheritance?

CRAFTS SUPPLIES FOR THE TORAH PORTION KORACH

SUPPLIES:
1. 12x12" Cardstock.
2. Green Felt.
3. Green Construction Paper.
4. Brown Cardstock.
5. White Construction Paper.
6. Yellow Construction Paper.
7. Gold Wrapping Paper.
8. Gems.
9. Almonds.

CRAFT INCLUDES ALMONDS!
PLEASE ASK IF THERE IS ANYONE WHO HAS ALLERGIES!!

CRAFTS: "Aaron's Budded Rod"

1. On 12×12" paper, glue pre-cut brown cardstock to represent the Rod.
2. On 2 lower branches, glue 2 pedals, one from green felt and one from green construction paper.

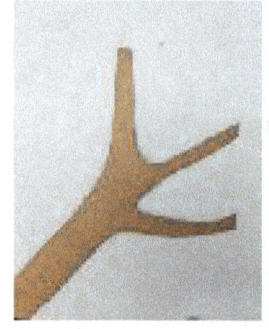

3. Glue yellow and white flowers.

4. Rip 3 small pieces of gold paper and crumple them into a ball. Then glue 1 at the center of each flower.

5. Take 2 pieces of almonds and glue them on the middle branch as shown.

Make sure there are no allergies!

6. If time allows, add gems on the flower pedals.

Chukkat-Balak

"Statute-Balak"

Torah Portions 39 & 40: Chukkat *"statute"* and Balak "Balak"

This week we have another combined Torah reading. The Torah portion titles are **Chukkat and Balak**. Chukkat means **'statute'** and is found in Numbers 19:2. Torah portion **'Balak' refers to the king of Moab** who summoned Balaam to curse the children of Israel. This is found in Numbers 22:2.

Numbers 19:2 TLV

"This is the **statute** of the Torah which Adonai commanded saying: Speak to Bnei-Yisrael that they bring to you a flawless red heifer on which there is no blemish and on which has never been a yoke..."

Numbers 22:2 TLV

When **Balak** son of Zippor, realized all that Bnei-Yisrael had done to the Amorites,..."

Scripture Readings:
Chukkat
Numbers 19:1-22:1, Judges 11:1-33, John 3:9-2, Psalm 95

Balak
Numbers 22:2-25:9, Micah 5:6-6:8, Matthew 21:1-11, Psalm 79

The Theme of the Torah Portion:
God Protects His People

Scripture for Theme

Numbers 22:12
"But God said to Balaam, "Do not go with them; you shall not curse the people, for they are blessed."

Torah Portion Outline

- Red Cow's Water of Purification, **Numbers 19:1-22**
- The Death of Miriam, **Numbers 20:1-6**
- Moses Strikes the Rock, **Numbers 20:7-13**
- No Passing Through the Land of Edom, **Numbers 20:14-21**
- The Death of Aaron, **Numbers 20:22-27**
- Israel Attacked by King of Canaan, **Numbers 21:1-3**
- Poisonous Snakes, **Numbers 21:4-9**
- Israel's Journey in the Wilderness, **Numbers 21:10-20**
- Victory Over the Canaanites, **Numbers 21:11-32**
- War With the King of Bashan, **Numbers 21:22:1**
- Balak Hires Balaam to Curse Israel, **Numbers 22:2-19**
- Balaam, the Talking Donkey, and the Angel, **Numbers 22:20-41**
- Blessings Over Israel Instead of a Curse, **Numbers 23:1-30**
- Balaam's Predicts Balak's Future, **Numbers 24:1-25**
- Israel's Forbidden Relationships With the Women of Moab, **Numbers 25:1-9**

LESSON SUMMARY

In the Torah portion of Chukkat, Moses was given the statute for the water of purification using the ashes of a three year old red heifer (female cow.) The water of purification was used to purify anyone who encountered a dead body. The purification process lasted for seven days. The cow was not to have had any spots, blemishes, defects, or even had a harness around its neck. We learn of Miriam's death, and the people cry for water. Adonai commanded Moses and Aaron to speak to the rock, but instead of speaking to the rock, Moses hit the rock twice with his staff. Moses was told he would not take the children of Israel into the land Adonai promised them because he and Aaron did not honor His name before the people when He hit the rock.

As they continued their journey from Kadesh to Edom, Moses sent messengers to the king for permission to pass through the land. The king did not permit them, so they turned around and journeyed toward Mount Hor. Shortly after, Adonai commanded Moses to take Aaron and his son Eleazar to the top of Mount Hor. Moses was instructed to take Aaron's priestly garments off of him, and put them on Eleazar. Aaron died on Mount Hor, and the people mourned his death for thirty days.

The children of Israel were attacked by Arad, the king of Canaan, and he captured some of them. The children of Israel prayed to Adonai and made a vow: "If you deliver this people into our hand, we will put their cities under the ban of destruction!" Adonai listened, and the people did just as they vowed. The name of the place was called Horamh. Then they traveled from Mount Hor along the route to the Sea of Reeds to go around the land of Edom, but the people became weary because of the long distance, so they spoke against Adonai and Moses. They even talked about how they hated eating the Manna. Adonai sent poisonous snakes among them and they bit the people, and many of them died. The people came to Moses and said, "We sinned when we spoke against Adonai and you! Pray to Adonai for us, that He may take away the snakes!" So Moses prayed for the people. Adonai said to Moses, "Make yourself a fiery snake and put it on a pole. Whenever anyone who has been bitten looks at it, he will live." So Moses made a bronze snake and put it on a pole, and it happened that whenever a snake bit anyone and he looked at the bronze snake, he lived (Numbers 22:7-9).

The Torah portion ended with the children of Israel singing a song of victory after Adonai gave them victory over Sihon, king of the Amorites, and Og, king of Bashan.

In the Torah reading, Balak, son of Zippor, and the people of Moab were terrified of the children of Israel because they heard what Israel had done to the Amorites. Moab said to the elders of Midian, "The multitude will lick up everything around us like the ox licks up the grass of the field (Numbers 22:4)." Balak sent messengers to Pethor to hire Balaam, son of Beor, to curse the children of Israel. When the elders came to Baalaam and told him the message from King Balak, he told them to spend the night and that he would inquire of Adonai to know what to do. That night, Adonai came to Balaam and told him not to go with them because Israel is blessed and he cannot curse them. The elders returned to Balak with Balaam's message, saying he could not come. Balak sent higher-ranking leaders with more money to Balaam. Adonai came to Balaam in the night and said to him that since the men came to get you to go with them, but speak only the words I tell you to speak.

The next morning, Balaam saddled his donkey, took with him two of his servants, and went with the men sent by the king. Adonai was angry with Balaam, so he sent an angel ahead of him to block his path. Balaam could not see the angel, but Adonai opened the donkey's eyes for him to see the angel. The angel stood in the way with his sword drawn. The donkey turned away from the angel two times on the road, and each time Balam hit the donkey with his stick. In turning away from the angel, the donkey crushed Balaam's foot against the wall. When the path was too narrow for the donkey to turn to the left or right, he lay down, and Balaam struck the donkey again. Adonai enabled the donkey to speak. She asked Balaam, "What have I done to you that you have hit me these three times" (Numbers 22:38)?

While Balaam and the donkey were talking, Adonai opened Balaam's eyes for him to see the angel that stood before them with his sword drawn. The angel told Balaam that if it wasn't for the donkey who turned away from Him these three times, He would have killed him already. Balaam said to the angel, "I have sinned; if this is displeasing to you, I will return home, but the angel said to him, Go with the men, but speak only what I tell you." Balaam went with the men. When Balak realized that Balaam had arrived, he met him in the city. He said to him, Didn't I send you an urgent request? Am I unable to pay my reward? Balaam responded, I am here now, but I can only speak the words God has put in my mouth to speak. Balak took Balaam to three different places for him to see the children of Israel and pronounce his curse. Through the words of Adonai, Balaam blessed the children of Israel three times. Balaak was angry with Balaam because he hired him to curse his enemies, but instead, he blessed them. Balaam also prophesied to Balak what the children of Israel would do to Moab.

Balaam reminded Balak that he told him he could only speak what God had told him to speak; then he went home, and so did Balak. The children of Israel stayed in the plains of Shittim. While staying in Shittim, they had forbidden relationships with the women of Moab. They were enticed by the women who invited them to worship their gods, eat foods offered to idols, and make sacrifices to them. The anger of Adonai rose against them, and a plague broke out among them. Adonai said to Moses, Gather all those responsible for leading the people astray and hang them. One of the men took his family and his Midianite woman to the Tent of Meeting before Moses, his brothers, and the whole assembly of the community while they were weeping. Phinehas, the son of Eleazar, saw them, got up from the crowd, took a spear, and thrust it through both the man and the woman in the man's tent. The plague was stopped, but 24,000 people died.

LESSON DISCUSSION

I CAN ONLY SPEAK THE WORDS OF ADONAI!

In this week's Torah portion, we learn about three nations that attacked the children of Israel. Adonai gave them the victory over all their enemies. Balak, son of Zippor, and the people of Moab were terrified of the children of Israel because they heard what Israel had done to the Amorites. Balak devised a plan to defeat the children of Israel, but his plan did not work.

Numbers 21:1-3 — Victory over the Canaanites
Numbers 21:21-25 — Victory over Sihon, King of the Amorites
Numbers 21:33-35 — Victory over Og, King of Bashan

Numbers 22:5-6 — Balak's Strategy to Defeat Israel
So he sent messengers to Balaam the son of Beor, at Pethor, which is near the Euphrates River, in the land of the sons of his people, to call for him, saying, "Behold, a people came out of Egypt; behold, they have covered the surface of the land, and they are living opposite me. **6** Now, therefore, please come, curse this people for me since they are too mighty for me; perhaps I will be able to defeat them and drive them out of the land. For I know that he whom you bless is blessed, and he whom you curse is cursed."

Three things Balak did not know:
1. Israel was, and is, blessed by Adonai and can not be cursed
2. Adonai fights for them, so fighting against them is fighting against Adonai
3. Only Adonai has the power to bless or curse

God's First Plan: Do Not Go!
Numbers 22:12-13
But God said to Balaam, "**Do not go with them; you shall not curse the people, for they are blessed.**" **13** So Balaam got up in the

morning and said to Balak's representatives, "Go back to your land, for the Lord has refused to let me go with you."

Balak sent messengers a second time to Balaam.
Numbers 22:18-19. — Even if Balak were to give me his house full of silver and gold, I could not do anything, either small or great, contrary to the command of the Lord my God. **19** Now please, you also stay here tonight, and I will find out **what else the Lord will say to me**.

Balaam's response revealed his heart. What else would Adonai speak to him? God's first instruction is always what He intends for us to follow. Balaam wanted to go for the money he had been promised.

Although it was not Adonai's will for Balaam to go with the men, He permitted him to go. Adonai told Balam, only the words I command you you must speak. **Numbers 22:20-21**

Balaam almost got killed by the angel of Adonai on his way to Balak. If it wasn't for his donkey that Adonai used to protect him, he would have died. Even when Adonai caused the donkey to speak, Balaam had no clue that Adonai was angry with him. Adonai opened Balaam's eyes to see the angel, but even then, his heart's desire was not to do what Adonai told him at first. **Numbers 22:22-41**

Do you want to be a part of Adonai's first plan or what He allows?

Three times Balaam attempted to curse Israel, but Adonai would not permit him. Balak was angry!

Numbers 24:10-14

Then Balak's anger burned against Balaam, and he struck his hands together; and Balak said to Balaam, "I called you to curse my enemies, but behold, you have persisted in blessing them these three times! **11** So flee to your place now. I said I would honor you greatly, but behold, the Lord has held you back from honor." **12** And Balaam said to Balak, "Did I not in fact tell your messengers whom you had sent to me, saying, **13** 'If Balak were to give me his house full of silver and gold, I could not do anything contrary to the command of the Lord, either good or bad, of my own accord. What the Lord speaks, I will speak'? **14** So now, behold, I am going to my people; come, and I will advise you of what this people will do to your people in the days to come."

Balaam was used by Adonai to bless Israel instead of cursing them, but he stood before them as an enemy of God representing Balak.

Who do you represent?
Don't allow others to make you speak negative words against someone else, or go places where you don't need to go.

Like Yeshua, our aim should be to do the will of the Father, speaking and doing only what pleases Him.

John 12: 49
For I have not spoken of Myself; but the Father who sent Me, He gave Me a commandment, what I should say and what I should speak.

2 Corinthians 5:20 CJB
Therefore we are ambassadors (representatives) of the Messiah; in effect, God is making his appeal through us. What we do is appeal on behalf of the Messiah, "Be reconciled to God!

TURNING POINT:

THE STRANGE LAW OF THE FEMALE COW: CHUKKAT

Do you always understand everything your parents or teachers tell you? NO? Well, it is that way with some of the commands of Adonai.

What is a chukkat? A chukkat is a statute or decree that Adonai commands us, but we don't know how to explain why He said to do it or not. It is usually something that does not make sense to us.

We know why we honor and keep the Shabbat. We can explain why we rest and don't do any work on the seventh day. Adonai rested from all his work on the seventh day, blessed the day, and called it holy. Therefore, He tells us to do the same. We cannot explain how the ashes of a red cow mixed with water purifies a person. We just have to believe it because that is what Adonai said would happen.

Numbers 19:4-12 — And Eleazar the priest shall take some of its blood with his finger and sprinkle some of its blood toward the front of the tent of meeting seven times. **5** Then the heifer shall be burned in his sight; its hide, its flesh, and its blood, with its refuse, shall be burned. **6** And the priest shall take cedar wood, hyssop, and scarlet material, and throw it into the midst of the burning heifer. **7** The priest shall then wash his clothes and bathe his body in water, and afterward come into the camp; but the priest will be unclean until evening. **8** The one who burns the heifer shall also wash his clothes in water and bathe his body in water, and will be unclean until evening. **9** Now a man who is clean shall gather up the ashes of the heifer and put them outside the camp in a clean place, and the congregation of the sons of Israel shall keep them for water to remove impurity; it is [h]purification from sin. **10** And the one who gathers the ashes of the heifer shall wash his clothes and will be unclean until evening; and it shall be a permanent statute for the sons of Israel and for the stranger who resides among them. **11** 'The one who touches the dead body of any person will also be unclean for seven days. **12** That one shall purify himself with the water on the third day and on the seventh day, and then he will be clean; but if he does not purify himself on the third day and on the seventh day, he will not be clean.

God's statute or decree for the water of purification with the ashes of the red heifer (female cow) was so Israel could maintain their purity whenever they encountered a dead body. It seems a little strange that Adonai would give this unusual method for the purification of the children of Israel after encountering a dead person, when we have read about so many people dying in previous Torah portions. Although this command is recorded in this Torah portion "Chukkat", the command was also given at Mount Sinai with all the other commandments that Moses received. This Torah portion records events that occurred almost 40 years after the spies brought back a bad report.

As you grow older, your friends or some family members may ask you questions about why you obey the Torah. Some questions you will answer with examples from the Torah. There will be some questions that you will have to respond to in faith, declaring that, "I obey by faith in Adonai through Yeshua." It requires us to have faith (trust in Adonai) to please Adonai.

Hebrews 11:6 CJB — And without trusting, it is impossible to be well pleasing to God, because whoever approaches him must trust that he does exist and that he becomes a Rewarder to those who seek him out.

TRUST IN ADONAI, even when it's hard the Ruach HaChodesh will give you strength to keep trusting Him.

PRACTICAL APPLICATIONS

Whose character am I expressing?
Balak - acted out of fear, cursing others
Balam - wanted fame and riches, blind to God's plan
Adonai - full of Mercy and Grace, Blesses His people

FOR CHILDREN 4-6 YEARS OLD
Parents help your child to identify which character he/she is expressing throughout the week.

FOR CHILDREN 7-12 YEARS OLD
Write the character of each person listed above and put it somewhere you can see it every day. At the end of each day, before you go to bed, ask yourself "Whose character did I express today?"

Pray and ask the Ruach HaChodesh to help you to always aim express the right character.

FOLLOW-UP FROM THE LAST TORAH PORTION
Ask who wants to share from last week's practical application LOVE LIKE MOSES.

FOR CHILDREN 4-6 YEARS OLD
When someone makes you feel angry or hurt, talk to your parents about it and let them help you do the right thing about it.

FOR CHILDREN 7-12 YEARS OLD
When others speak badly about you, ask the Holy Spirit to help you respond in love knowing you are Adonai's son/daughter, and you were chosen to lead by example, not to follow the crowd.

QUESTIONS - TEACHERS ANSWER KEY

1. Why weren't Moses and Aaron allowed to enter the promised land?
They did not honor the name of Adonai and speak to the rock as He had instructed them. Moses hit the rock twice instead.

2. On which Mountain did Aaron die?
Mount Hor

3. Who was given the priestly garment after Aaron's death?
Eleazar Aaron's son

4. Who was hired to curse Israel and by whom was he hired?
Balaam was hired by Balak, King of Moab

5. What was Adonai's first answer to Balaam?
Do not go, the people are blessed and you cannot curse them

6. Why did the donkey turn off the road?
He saw the angel of Adonai standing with his sword drawn

7. What did the donkey do that was unusual?
She spoke to Balaam

8. How many times did Balaam bless Israel?
Three times

9. Why did Adonai send poisonous snakes that bit the people?
They grumbled and complained about how they hated eating Manna

10. How were they healed from the snake bites?
Looking at the bronze snake Adonai told Moses to make and put it on a pole

11. In your own words, explain what a "chukkat" or "statute" of Adonai is.
Answers will vary

QUESTIONS - CHILDREN'S COPY

1. Why weren't Moses and Aaron allowed to enter the promised land?

2. On which Mountain did Aaron die?

3. Who was given the priestly garment after Aaron's death?

4. Who was hired to curse Israel and by whom was he hired?

5. What was Adonai's first answer to Balaam?

6. Why did the donkey turn off the road?

7. What did the donkey do that was unusual?

8. How many times did Balaam bless Israel?

9. Why did Adonai send poisonous snakes that bit the people?

10. How were they healed from the snake bites?

11. In your own words, explain what a "chukkat" or "statute" of Adonai is.

CRAFTS SUPPLIES FOR THE TORAH PORTION CHUKAT-BALAK

SUPPLIES:
1. 12x12" Cardstock.
2. White 8 ½×11" Cardstock.
3. Paper Fastener.
4. Doll Eyes.
5. Glue and Glue Sticks.
6. Coloring Supplies.
7. Gems.

CRAFTS: ANGEL AND THE DONKEY

1. Glue the head to the body.

2. Glue the tail.

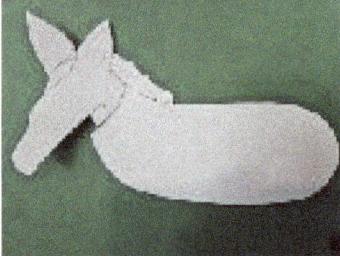 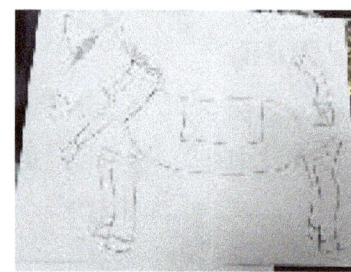

3. Glue legs to the body.

 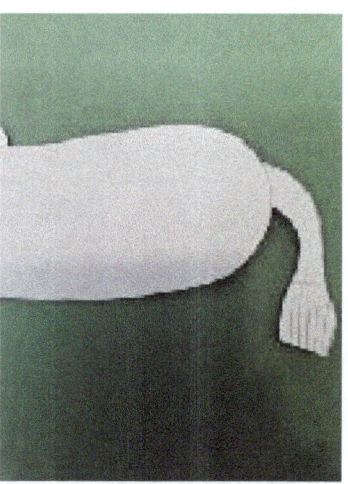

4. Attach the bottom jaw with a paper fastener and stick the doll's eyes.

5. Color the donkey's mane and ears.
6. Color and decorate the saddle.
7. Glue the donkey as shown on the cardstock. Do NOT GLUE the bottom jaw so it can move up and down.

8. Color the ANGEL.
9. Glue him to the cardstock so his hand is touching the donkey's head.
10. Write on top: "The Talking Donkey!?"

Pinchas

"Phinehas"

Torah Portion 41: Pinchas "Phinehas"

The title of this week's Torah Portion reading is **Pinchas**, which is the Hebrew name for **Phinehas**. Phinehas is the name of Eleazar's son who turned away the anger of the Adonai against the children of Israel. His name is mentioned in the second verse of our Torah Portion reading.

Numbers 25:11 NASB

Then the Lord spoke to Moses, saying, **11** "***Phinehas*** the son of Eleazar, the son of Aaron the priest, has turned away My wrath from the sons of Israel in that he was jealous with My jealousy among them, so that I did not destroy the sons of Israel in My jealousy.

Scripture Readings:

Numbers 25:10-29:40, Jeremiah 1:1-23, John 2:13-22, Psalm 50

The Theme of the Torah Portion:

Honoring the Father

Scripture for Theme

Numbers 27:12-14 TLV

Then Adonai said to Moses, "Go up this mountain of the Abarim range and look at the land that I have given to Bnei-Yisrael. **13** When you have seen it, you will be gathered to your people, just as Aaron your brother was gathered. **14** For in the wilderness of Zin during the strife of the community, you both rebelled against My Word instead of honoring Me as holy at the waters before their eyes." (These were the waters of Meribah at Kadesh in the wilderness of Zin.)

Torah Portion Outline

- The Righteousness of Phinehas, **Numbers 25:10-18**
- Israel's Counting of the Second Generation, **Numbers 26:1-51**
- The Dividing of the Land by Lots, **Numbers 26:52-56**
- The Counting of the Levites, **Numbers 26:57-65**
- Laws for the Inheritance of the Land, **Numbers 27:1-12**
- Joshua, the Next Leader, **Numbers 27:13-23**
- Laws for the Daily Offerings, **Numbers 28:1-8**
- Sabbath and Its Offerings, **Numbers 28:9-10**
- Laws for the Monthly Offerings, **Numbers 28:11-15**
- Offerings for Passover, **Numbers 28:16-25**
- Offerings for Shavuot, **Numbers 28:26-31**
- Offerings for Feast of Trumpets, **Numbers 29:1-6**
- Offerings for Day of Atonement, **Numbers 29:7-11**
- Offerings for Sukkot, **Numbers 29:12-30:1**

LESSON SUMMARY

Last week's Torah Portion ended with the courage of Phinehas, who, by his actions, stopped the plague from Adonai because some of the men joined the women of Moab and Midian in unholy relationships. Adonai declared in this week's Torah portion that He has established a covenant for peace with Phinehas and his descendants forever because he honored God and made atonement for his people.

The Torah portion continues with the instructions Adonai gives Moses for the second generation of Israel. These are the children of all the adults who listened to the bad reports of the spies and died in the wilderness after forty years. All except Caleb and Joshua died. Adonai told Moses to take a count of all the sons twenty years of age and older for war, just as he did with their parents. The total number of sons of Israel counted for war was 601,730. The Levites were not counted with the men for war, but were counted for the priesthood. Every male was counted from one month of age and older. The total number of Levites counted was 23,000.

Instructions were given to Moses for how the land was to be divided among the tribes for their inheritance. They received their inheritance according to their names. The tribes with a large number of people were given a larger portion of the land than the smaller tribes with fewer people. Each tribe was given an inheritance according to the number of people, except the tribe of Levi. The Levites did not receive any land as their inheritance because Adonai was their inheritance and portion. Among the tribes, there was a man from the family of Manasseh who had no sons. He had five daughters. They went to Moses and asked that their father's portion of the inheritance be given to them to preserve his name among his family. Moses took their request to Adonai. Adonai responded that they were right; they should receive their father's inheritance. It became a Torah law that if a man had no sons, his daughter would receive his inheritance.

Adonai also spoke to Moses and told him to go up to Mount Abiram and see the promised land, for he too would not enter it, but die like his brother Aaron did on Mount Hor. Moses had rebelled against the command of Adonai to honor His name before the people in the wilderness of Zin when they complained about not having any water. Adonai had told Moses to speak to the rock for water to flow, but he hit the rock twice instead. Moses, unable to lead the people into the promised land, asked Adonai to appoint a man to lead the people as they go out and come in, so that they would not be like sheep without a shepherd. Adonai chose Joshua to lead the people. Joshua was filled with the Spirit of wisdom. He was presented before Eleazar the priest, and all the congregation.

Adonai reminded the children of Israel about the requirements of the offerings that were to be presented to him: the daily offerings, the sabbath offerings, the monthly (new moon) offerings, and the offerings that were to be offered on the appointed feast days.

LESSON DISCUSSION

Honor the Father:

Phinehas honored Adonai:
Numbers 25:10-13 MSG
10-13 God spoke to Moses: "Phinehas son of Eleazar, son of Aaron the priest, has stopped my anger against the People of Israel. Because he was as zealous for my honor as I myself am, I didn't kill all the People of Israel in my zeal. So tell him that I am making a Covenant-of-Peace with him. He and his descendants are joined in a covenant of eternal priesthood, because he was zealous for his God and made atonement for the People of Israel."

Phinehas and his descendants received a covenant inheritance of eternal peace because he honored Adonai.

Moses was given instructions to divide the promised land by lots among the sons of Israel by tribes. In the tribe of Manasseh, there was a man who had no sons, only daughters.

What will happen to his inheritance?
The daughters of Zelophehad honored their father and they received his inheritance.

Numbers 27:1-7 TLV
The daughters of Zelophehad son of Hepher son of Gilead son of Machir son of Manasseh, of the families of Manasseh son of Joseph (the names of his daughters were Mahlah, Noah, Hoglah, Milcah, and Tirzah) **2** stood before Moses, Eleazar the kohen and the princes of the entire assembly at the entrance to the Tent of Meeting and said,
3 "Our father died in the wilderness. But he was not one of the followers banding together against Adonai with Korah, though he died for his own sin. Yet he had no sons. **4** Why should our father's name

diminish from his family just because he had no son? Give to us property among our father's brothers." **5** So Moses brought their issue before Adonai, **6** and Adonai spoke to Moses saying, **7** "The daughters of Zelophehad are right in saying you should give them property by inheritance among their father's relatives. You are to turn over the inheritance of their father to them."

From previous Torah portions, we see the results of not honoring Adonai.

The spies who returned with a bad report about the promised land and everyone who believed them, not Adonai, died and didn't enter the promised land. Korah and all those who joined in his rebellion against Adonai also died in the presence of Adonai. Aaron and Moses also had to accept the consequences of not honoring the name of Adonai.

Numbers 27:12-14

Then the Lord said to Moses, "Go up to this mountain of Abarim, and see the land which I have given to the sons of Israel. **13** When you have seen it, you too will be gathered to your people, as Aaron your brother was; **14** for in the wilderness of Zin, during the strife of the congregation, you rebelled against My command to treat Me as holy before their eyes at the water." (These are the waters of Meribah of Kadesh in the wilderness of Zin.)

In everything we do, Adonai desires for us to honor His name Deuteronomy 6:5, Colossians 3:17, Proverbs 3:9

Colossians 3:17

Whatever you do in word or deed, do all in the name of the Lord Jesus, giving thanks through Him to God the Father.

Like the daughters of Zelophehad honored their father, we should honor our parents. Exodus 20:12, Ephesians 6:1-3

- **Ephesians 6:1**

Children, obey your parents in the Lord, for this is right. **2** Honor your father and mother (which is the first commandment with a promise), **3** so that it may be well with you, and that you may live long on the earth.

Yeshua our Example

Yeshua honored the Father in everything He said and did. **John 12:49-50**

Even in His death, Yeshua honored His Father.
Philippians 2:8-11

Being found in appearance as a man, He humbled Himself by becoming obedient to the point of death, even death [c]on a cross. **9** For this reason also, God highly exalted Him, and bestowed on Him the name which is above every name, **10** so that at the name of Jesus every knee will bow, of those who are in heaven and on earth and under the earth, **11** and that every tongue will confess that Jesus Christ is Lord, to the glory of God the Father.

John 12:26 — "If any of you wants to serve me, then follow me. Then you'll be where I am, ready to serve at a moment's notice. The Father will honor and reward anyone who serves me.

TURNING POINT:

The Next Generation Leader

The children of Israel were once again getting ready to enter the promised land. All those who rebelled against Adonai after hearing the bad report the spies brought back died. Adonai honored His word, the promise He made to preserve Caleb and Joshua's lives because they honored Him when they went to spy out the land.

Moses did not enter the land or lead the children of Israel because he did not honor the name of Adonai in the wilderness of Zin when the people quarreled for water. However, Moses asked the Lord to appoint another man who would lead the people so they would not be like sheep without a shepherd. " Moses spoke to Adonai, saying, "May Adonai, God of the spirits of all flesh, appoint a man over the community to go out and come in before them, who will lead them out and bring them out so that the people of Adonai will not be like sheep without a shepherd." Numbers 27:15-17TLV

Adonai chose Joshua as the next leader. Who was Joshua? The Torah tells us that Joshua was the son of Nun, from the tribe of Ephraim. What else do we know about him from reading? Joshua was Moses' assistant. He was the only one with Moses on top of Mount Sinai when Moses received the Ten Commandments (Exodus 32:15–18). Joshua was the one who remained in the Tent of Meeting in the presence of Adonai when Adonai had a meeting with Miriam and Aaron because they spoke against Moses (Exodus 33:11).

What can we learn from the life of Joshua?
- You have to learn to follow before you can lead
- You need the Spirit of Adonai to be an effective leader
- A leader is chosen by Adonai, not self-appointed
- A leader is given authority by Adonai and his Predecessor
- A leader does not lead according to his own plan, but according to Adonai's plan

Do you desire to become a leader? Submit to those in authority and learn from them. Ask the Lord to show you the person who can be a Godly example for you to follow.

LEAD LIKE JOSHUA!

PRACTICAL APPLICATIONS

Honor the Father in your actions.

Learning to serve like Joshua - assist before you can lead others.

FOR CHILDREN 4-6 YEARS OLD

Ask your parents how you can help them when they are:
- Preparing dinner
- Cleaning the house
- Packing away the groceries
- Folding the laundry

FOR CHILDREN 7-12 YEARS OLD

As children of Adonai, we are all called to lead by example.

Learn to lead when you are at home and school. Be an example in your speech and your actions toward others.

Ask the Lord to show you the person who can be a Godly example for you to follow.

FOLLOW-UP FROM THE LAST TORAH PORTION

Ask who wants to share from last week's practical application.

Whose character am I expressing?

Balak - acted out of fear, cursing others
Balam - wanted fame and riches, blind to God's plan
Adonai - full of Mercy and Grace, Blesses His people

FOR CHILDREN 4-6 YEARS OLD

Parents help your child to identify which character he/she is expressing throughout the week.

FOR CHILDREN 7-12 YEARS OLD

Write the character of each person listed above and put it where you can see it daily. At the end of each day, before you go to bed, ask yourself "Whose character did I express today?"

Pray and ask the Ruach HaKodesh to help you always to express the right character.

QUESTIONS - TEACHERS ANSWER KEY

1. **With whom did Adonai make a covenant of peace?**
   Phinehas

2. **What was the name of the man who had no sons?**
   Zelophehad

3. **Name three of his daughters.**
   Noah, Hoglah, Milcah, tirzah, Mahlah

4. **What was the question the daughters of Zelophehad asked Moses?**
   Why should our father's name diminish from his family because he had no sons?

5. **What was the total number of men counted for war?**
   603, 730

6. **How was the land divided for an inheritance?**
   By names, or tribes

7. **Which tribe was not counted for war or received land as an inheritance?**
   Levi

8. **Where did Moses go to see the promised land?**
   On Mount Abiram

9. **Who was chosen to lead the next generation?**
   Joshua

10. **Who was the priest who stood to pray with Joshua?**
    Eleazar

QUESTIONS - CHILDREN'S COPY

1. With whom did Adonai make a covenant of peace?

2. What was the name of the man who had no sons?

3. Name three of his daughters

4. What was the question the daughters of Zelophehad asked Moses?

5. What was the total number of men counted for war?

6. How was the land divided for an inheritance?

7. Which tribe was not counted for war or received land as an inheritance?

8. Where did Moses go to see the promised land?

9. Who was chosen to lead the next generation?

10. Who was the priest who stood to pray with Joshua?

CRAFTS SUPPLIES FOR THE TORAH PORTION PINCHAS

SUPPLIES:
1. 12x12" Cardstock of Various Colors.
2. 12x12" Brown Cardstock.
3. Color Construction Paper.
4. Swatches, 180 Pieces Cotton Fabric.
5. Colorful Pipe Cleaners.
6. Dolls Eyes.
7. Print Paper.
8. Glue and Glue Sticks.
9. Double-sided Tape.
10. Coloring supplies

CRAFTS: "Daughters of Tzelafchad"

1. Ask children to glue the pre-cut cardstock of 5 dolls, as shown.
2. Ask each child to choose 5 swatches for each doll for a skirt. Swatches are already prepared as shown.
3. Glue them on.

4. Glue 5 pre-cut shirts on each doll. Try to follow the same overlap as the original artwork.

5. With double-sided tape, attach pre-cut and bent pipe cleaners to the heads to represent hair - as shown.
6. Glue googly eyes on each doll.
7. Draw noses and mouths.
8. Color the header and glue it on top.
9. Glue the names of each daughter under each doll.

THE FINISHED WORK

Mattot-Massei

"Tribes-Journeys"

Torah Portions 42 & 43: Mattot "Tribes" and "Massei "Journeys"

This week's Torah reading combines two Torah Portions. The first Torah portion is **Mattot** meaning *tribes*, which is found in Number 30:1. The second Torah portion is **Massei** meaning *journeys*, which is found in Number 33:1.

Numbers 30:1

Then Moses spoke to the heads of the **tribes** of the sons of Israel, saying, "This is the word which the Lord has commanded.

Numbers 33:1

These are the **journeys** of the sons of Israel, by which they came out from the land of Egypt by their armies, under the leadership of Moses and Aaron.

Scripture Readings:

Mattot - Numbers 30:1-32:42, Jeremiah 1:1-2:3, Matthew 5:33-37, Psalm 111

Massei - Number 33:1-36:13, Jeremiah 2:2-28, Mark 11:12-25, Psalm 49

The Theme of the Torah Portion:

Vengeance belongs to Adonai

Scripture for Theme

Numbers 32:3

Moses spoke to the people, saying, "Arm men from among you for the war, that they may go against Midian to execute the Lord's vengeance on Midian.

Torah Portion Outline

- Making a Vow, **Numbers 30:1-3**
- When a Young Woman Makes a Vow, **Numbers 30:4-6**
- When a Married Woman Makes a Vow, **Numbers 30:7-16**
- Adonai's Vengeance Against Midian, **Numbers 31:1-18**
- Purification After War, **Numbers 31:19-24**
- Dividing the Plunder From War, **Numbers 31:25-47**
- An Offering to Adonai, **Numbers 31:48-54**
- Two and a Half Tribes Inherit Gilead, **Numbers 32:1-42**
- Israel's Journey Through the Wilderness, **Numbers 33.1-49**
- Laws for Possessing the Land, **Numbers 33:50-56**
- The Borders of the Land of Israel, **Numbers 34:1-15**
- Leaders to Assign the Land of Inheritance, **Numbers 34:16-29**
- Cities for the Levites to Live, **Numbers 35:1-5**
- Cities of Refuge, **Numbers 35:6-15**
- Who Can Enter or Not Enter the City of Refuge, **Numbers 35:16-29**
- Don't Accept a Ransom for Murder, **Numbers 35:30-34**
- Inheritance by Marriage, **Numbers 36:1-13**

LESSON SUMMARY

This week's Torah reading combines two Torah portions: Mattot, which means tribes, and Massei, which means journeys. In the Torah portion, Mattot, Moses received Adonai's instructions for when a man or woman make a vow. If a man makes a vow, he should make sure he fulfills his vow. If a woman makes a vow while she still lives with her father, he can cancel or approve her vow immediately when he learns about it. The same principle is applied to a woman when she is married and makes a vow. Her husband has the right to cancel or approve her vow immediately when he learns about it. However, Adonai declares that a widow or divorced woman is held accountable for her vow and must fulfill it.

Adonai declared that the children of Israel should take His vengeance against the Midianites because, with the help of Balaam, they led Israel into idolatry and harlotry. A thousand men were sent from each tribe to war. The sons of Israel went to war with Midain, led by Phinehas and Eleazar the priests, with the holy vessels, and the two silver trumpets for sounding an alarm. The Lord gave them victory. They killed all the men and burned the cities. They also killed Balaam and the five kings of Midian. They took captive the women and children of Midian. They plundered Midian and took their livestock, gold, silver, bronze tin, iron, and all their material possessions. They brought everything back with them. Moses, Eleazar the priest, and the leaders met them outside the camp. Moses was angry with the men because they spared the women, who caused the sons of Israel to worship idols and turn away from Adonai. The men who went to war and all those they had captured had to purify themselves. Adonai required anyone who encountered a dead body to purify themselves with the water of purification on the third day and seventh day before they could enter the camp. All the articles of gold, silver, bronze, tin, lead, iron, and fabric also had to be purified before they could enter the camp. Then all the plunder was divided between those who went to war and those who were in the camp. The soldiers and the congregation paid tax from their portion of the plunder. It was given to the Levites. Not one man died among the children of Israel who went to war. The commanders brought an offering of thanksgiving to Adonai for His protection. They brought gold and fine jewelry weighing about six hundred pounds.

The sons of Reuben and Gad had many farm animals. When they realized that the land of Jazer and Gilead was good for rearing animals, they requested to settle there instead of going across the Jordan into the land of Canaan, which Adonai promised. Moses was angry with them at first because he thought they were trying to discourage the hearts of their brothers as the spies did and hindered them from entering the land. Reuben and Gad, however, assured him that they would set up their camp to protect their wives and children, and they would arm themselves and go before their brothers across the Jordan and help them settle in the land of their inheritance before returning home. Moses agreed to let them settle, but he warned them, "If you will not do so, behold, you have sinned against the Lord, and be sure your sin will find you out" (Numbers 31:23). He also gave half the tribe of Manasseh a part of the inheritance with Reuben and Gad.

In the Torah Portion, Massei, Moses reviews the journeys of the children of Israel from the day they left Egypt. Israel made forty-two journeys in the wilderness from Rameses, Egypt. They left Egypt on the fifteenth day of Nisan (the first month) until they camped by the Jordan in the plains of Moab, opposite Jericho. They made one journey comprised of multiple pit stops. Adonai gave instructions for when they were to cross the Jordan into the land of Canaan. Adonai instructed them: "You shall drive out all the inhabitants of the land from before you, and destroy all their figured stones, and destroy all their molten images, and demolish all their high places; and you shall take possession of the land and live in it, for I have given the land to you to possess it." Numbers 33:52-53. Adonai also warned them: "But if you do not drive out the inhabitants of the land from before you, then it shall come about that those whom you let remain of them will become as pricks in your eyes and as thorns in your sides, and they will trouble you in the land in which you live. And as I plan to do to them, so I will do to you." Numbers 33:55-56. In addition, the children of Israel received the borders to which the land of their inheritance extended; from the South, East, North, and West. The land of Canaan (the promised land) was allotted to the remaining nine and a half tribes. The sons of Reuben and Gad and the half-tribe of Manasseh had already received their inheritance "across the Jordan opposite Jericho, eastward towards the sunrise (Numbers 34:15)."

Leaders were appointed from each tribe to assist Eleazar the priest and Joshua to apportion the land for inheritance. The sons of Israel were commanded to give the Levites cities and farmland to live in from their inheritance. The Levites were also to get six cities of refuge for anyone who unintentionally killed someone. The Levites were to receive forty-eight cities; forty-two for them to live in and six cities for refuge. The sons of Israel were also to select for themselves cities of refuge for anyone who unintentionally killed a person. They were to choose six cities; three across the Jordan, and three in the land of Canaan. The cities were intended for the sons of Israel, foreigners, and those among them who had unintentionally killed a person; who was fleeing from those seeking revenge.

As the Torah portion comes to a close, the sons of Gilead, the son of Machir, the son of Manasseh, and the families of the sons of Joseph, spoke to Moses about Adonai's command to give the daughters of Zelophehad their inheritance. They explained to Moses that should the daughters marry anyone from among the other eleven (11) tribes during the Jubilee, their inheritance would be added to the tribe from which their husband belongs. The inheritance of our fathers would become smaller. Moses brought their concern to Adonai. Adonai responded, "The sons of Joseph are right in their statement" (Numbers 36:5). Adonai commanded that the daughters of Zelophehad could marry anyone they desired as long as they married within their father's tribe so that the possession of their inheritance would not transfer from one tribe to another.

Praise Adonai we have completed another book in the Torah!
Chazak, Chazak V'nit Chazek!
Be Strong, Be Strong, and May We Be Strengthened!

LESSON DISCUSSION

CAUTIONS FOR THE LAND: MAKING A VOW AND DEFILING THE LAND

Numbers 30:1-2

Moses spoke to the princes of the tribes of Bnei-Yisrael saying, "This is what Adonai has commanded: **2** Whenever a man makes a vow to Adonai or swears an oath to obligate himself by a pledge, he is not to violate his word but do everything coming out of his mouth.

Adonai cautions the people about making a vow. Why?
When we make a vow and do not fulfill our vow, we sin against Adonai.

Ecclesiastes 5: 4-6

When you vow a vow to God, don't defer to pay it; for he has no pleasure in fools. Pay that which you vow. **5** It is better that you should not vow, than that you should vow and not pay. **6** Don't allow your mouth to lead you into sin. Don't protest before the messenger that this was a mistake. Why should God be angry at your voice, and destroy the work of your hands?

Moses gave the same warning to the son of the tribes of Reuben and Gad. The tribes wanted to settle in Gilead instead of going into the promised land. They promised to arm themselves, go before their brothers across the Jordan, and help the rest of the tribes possess the promised land.

Numbers 32:16-19 TLV

Then they came up to him and said, "We will build sheepfolds for our livestock and cities for our children. **17** But we are prepared to arm ourselves and go ahead of Bnei-Yisrael until we have brought them to their place. Our children will live in the cities fortified against the inhabitants of the land. **18** We will not return to our homes until each one of Bnei-Yisrael has received his inheritance. **19** Yet we will not inherit with them on the side beyond the Jordan, since our inheritance has come on the east side of the Jordan."

Moses told them if they did as they promised then the land of Gilead would be theirs to possess but if they did not, they sin against Adonai.

Numbers 32:20-24 TLV
Moses said to them, "If you will do this—if you will arm yourselves for battle for Adonai, **21** and if all of you cross the Jordan until Adonai has driven His enemies from before Him **22** and the land is subdued before Adonai—then afterward you may return and be free before Adonai and Israel. Then this territory will be your possession before Adonai. **23** "But if you don't do this, behold, you sin against Adonai! Be assured! Your sin will find you out! **24** Build for yourselves cities for your children and pens for your flocks. Then do what has come out of your mouth."

Yeshua also warns us about making vows
Matthew 5:34-37 WEB
But I tell you, don't swear at all: neither by heaven, for it is the throne of God; **35** nor by the earth, for it is the footstool of his feet; nor by Jerusalem, for it is the city of the great King. **36** Neither shall you swear by your head, for you can't make one hair white or black.
37 But let your 'Yes' be 'Yes' and your 'No' be 'No.' Whatever is more than these is of the evil one.

Adonai Dwells Among His People.
Adonai gave two orders to the children of Israel in this week's Torah readings. The first order is about making a vow, and the second is not to defile the land. These two orders may not seem connected, but as we look at these warnings, we will realize that they are connected.

When we don't fulfill our vows, we sin against Adonai. Where there is sin, Adonai cannot dwell.

Adonai told the children of Israel that when they possess the land, they should choose cities to be cities of refuge for anyone who unintentionally kills another. This way, he will remain alive until he goes before the people to be tried for his sin. Adonai warns them not to take a bribe from someone guilty of murder so he might be freed, nor are they to take a bribe from the innocent so he might be put to death. The city of refuge is for the innocent, and he needed to live there until the death of the priest. **(Reference Numbers 35)**

Numbers 35:33-34 NASB
So you shall not pollute the land in which you are; for blood pollutes the land and no expiation can be made for the land for the blood that is shed on it, except by the blood of him who shed it. **34** You shall not defile the land in which you live, in the midst of which I dwell; for I the Lord am dwelling in the midst of the sons of Israel.'"

If we desire for Adonai to dwell with us we cannot pollute His dwelling place.

1 Corinthians 3:16 NASB
Do you not know that you are a temple of God and that the Spirit of God dwells in you?

TURNING POINT:

BORDER PATROL: PROTECTING YOUR INHERITANCE

Adonai gave specific instructions for the borders of the land that the children of Israel were to possess for their inheritance. He also gave instructions for how the land was to be divided among the tribes. The children of Israel were to drive out all the people from the land.

Numbers 33: 50-53 MSG

God spoke to Moses on the Plains of Moab at Jordan-Jericho: "Tell the People of Israel, When you cross the Jordan into the country of Canaan, drive out the native population before you, destroy their carved idols, destroy their cast images, level their worship-mounds so that you take over the land and make yourself at home in it; I've given it to you. It's yours.

Adonai told them what they should do to possess the land and live in peace

- drive out the native population
- destroy their carved idols
- destroy their cast images
- level their worship-mounds

The most important thing for the children of Israel was their obedience to the word of Adonai. Adonai declared to them if they did not obey, "But if you don't drive out the native population, everyone you let stay there will become a cinder in your eye and a splinter in your foot. They'll give you endless trouble right in your own backyards. And I'll start treating you the way I planned to treat them." (Numbers 33: 55-56 MSG)

It is the same for those who believe in Yeshua. If you want to receive Adonai's blessings, you have to learn to obey and follow His instructions.

How do you protect your inheritance?
- Do not keep friends with those who don't want to serve Adonai
- Don't make idols of the things you own (loving them more than Adonai)
- Don't watch or listen to things that pollute Adonai's temple (your body)
- Worship Adonai only

BE A BORDER PATROL, PROTECT YOUR INHERITANCE!

John 15:16
"You did not choose Me (Yeshua), but I chose you. I selected you so that you would go and produce fruit, and your fruit would remain. Then the Father will give you whatever you ask in My name.

PRACTICAL APPLICATIONS

Taking Responsibility for Your Actions: Yes or No

FOR CHILDREN 5-8 YEARS OLD

If you get in trouble this week don't try to make excuses for your actions. Admit you are wrong and ask for forgiveness.

FOR CHILDREN 9-12 YEARS OLD

When you do something that is not acceptable to your parents or teachers, don't try to explain or make excuses for your actions. Admit you're wrong and ask for forgiveness.

When your friend asks you to do something. Do not make a promise if you are not able to keep your promise. Always ask your parents' permission before making a promise to a friend.

FOLLOW-UP FROM THE LAST TORAH PORTION

Ask who wants to share from last week's practical application.

Honor the Father in your actions.
Learning to serve like Joshua - assist before you can lead others.

FOR CHILDREN 4-6 YEARS OLD

Ask your parents how you can help them when they are:
- Preparing dinner
- Cleaning the house
- Packing away the grocery
- Folding the laundry

FOR CHILDREN 7-12 YEARS OLD

As children of Adonai, we are all called to lead by example.

Learn to lead when you are at home and school. Be an example in your speech and in your actions toward others.

Ask the Lord to show you the person who can be a Godly example for you to follow.

QUESTIONS - TEACHERS ANSWER KEY

1. **Who has the right to cancel a woman's vow to Adonai?**
   Father or husband

2. **Where were the children of Israel camped?**
   By the Jordan / plains of Moab

3. **On which nation did Adonai declare vengeance?**
   Midian

4. **Who was killed along with the 5 kings of Midian?**
   Balaam

5. **Name the tribes who chose their inheritance.**
   Reuben and Gad

6. **How many pitstops along the journey did Israel make in the wilderness?**
   Forty-two (42)

7. **How many tribes inherited the promised land?**
   Nine and a half

8. **How many men were sent from each tribe to war?**
   One thousand from each tribe

9. **Who led the men out to war?**
   Phinehas and Eleazar

10. **What was Eleazar carrying?**
    The holy vessels and the two silver trumpets

QUESTIONS - CHILDREN'S COPY

1. Who has the right to cancel a woman's vow to Adonai?

2. Where were the children of Israel camped?

3. On which nation did Adonai declare vengeance?

4. Who was killed along with the 5 kings of Midian?

5. Name the tribes who chose their inheritance.

6. How many pitstops along the journey did Israel make in the wilderness?

7. How many tribes inherited the promised land?

8. How many men were sent from each tribe to war?

9. Who led the men out to war?

10. What was Eleazar carrying?

CRAFTS SUPPLIES FOR THE TORAH PORTION MATTOT-MASSEI

SUPPLIES:
1. White Cardstock.
2. Print Plain Paper.
3. Markers, Crayons, Pencils.
4. Glue Sticks.

CRAFTS: THE LAND OF 12 TRIBES PUZZLE

Children will put together a puzzle on how the land was divided and placed for the 12 tribes in the Holy Land. They will have colored examples to refer to.

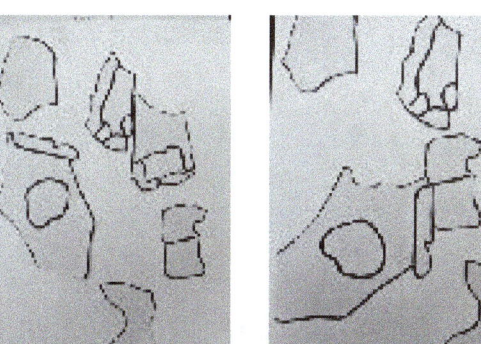

1. Children will receive black and white pieces of a puzzle. They will start assembling the puzzle.
2. Children will need to glue pieces to cardstock to finish assembling.

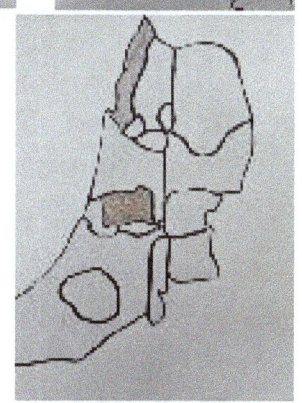

3. Once the puzzle is complete, start coloring each tribe a different color.
4. After coloring is done, mark them with the correct names.

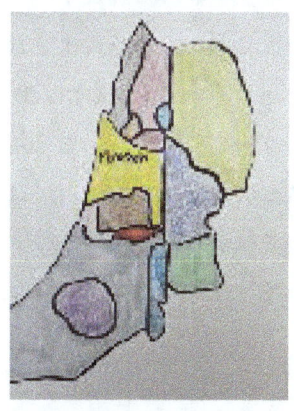

5. Then finish with marking surrounding territories as shown.

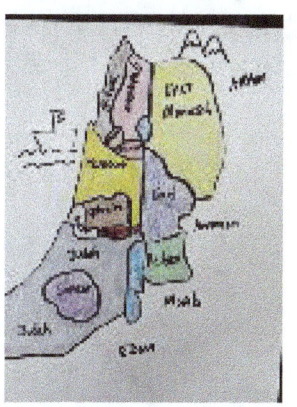

About the Authors

Natalee Henry began her personal faith journey in 1996 with a burning desire to live an extraordinary life for the Lord. Since then, the Lord has kindled a passion within her for sharing and teaching the Word of God.

In 2016, God answered Natalee's prayer for spiritual growth when she was introduced to studying, learning, and implementing the Torah way of life as a believer in Yeshua. Natalee is a Torah-observant believer learning to honor God's Appointed Times and serving within her local congregation to all ages.

Natalee is an author, motivational speaker, and founder of the Season Destiny Ministry designed to "*empower youths to make the right decisions in life.*" Natalee is a graduate of International Seminary Bible College, and authored **Seasons of Life-Taking Man Back To God**, 2005; **Embracing Destiny**, 2010; **Overcome to Fulfill Your Purpose: Become Successfully You**, and **Successfully You, Leadership Training Workbook** 2018, and her most recent, **Making Transition Through Crisis: A Rebuilding Guide for Young Professionals**, 2021.

Natalee has a passion for young people and seeks to share with them that they do not have to 'settle' for being less than God created them to be; nor do they need to succumb to today's culture, lies, and worldliness.

 **Yevgeniya Calendrillo** was born and raised in Ukraine to a secular Jewish family. Growing up, Yevgeniya yearned for a relationship with God for many years. By the age of 24, she was married and living in the United States. Yevgeniya and her husband are entrepreneurs and business partners selling their artwork and also are heavily focused on nutrition and health. Yevgeniya and her husband have one son, whom she homeschooled for 3 1/2 years.

Yevgeniya was invited to a Messianic congregation in Brooklyn where she accepted Yeshua as her Savior; and opened the Bible for the very first time. Yevgeniya has been a Messianic believer for over 20 years.

Yevgniya has a Bachelor's degree in Fashion Design from the Fashion Institute of Technology, New York. Yevgeniya has many years of experience in the New York fashion industry. Yevgniya is an artist who is gifted in watercolor painting. She recently discovered her talent for children's crafts and utilizes her knowledge, and experience in arts and design, as tools for investing in children for the Kingdom of God. Yevgeniya is currently serving as Children's Ministry Leader and a children's Torah teacher at Save The Nations.

Yevgeniya has a passion to follow God, to be obedient to His Torah instructions, to seek Him diligently, and to walk in her calling to teach Torah and Hebrew lessons to children.

About the Book

BaMidbar (Book 4: Numbers) is a part of the Torah Curriculum for children, covering the first five books of the Bible. This curriculum is based on the weekly Torah Portions so they may learn Torah in a simple and practical way.

The Lessons are structured so our children will learn from the Torah Portions and see the connection with Yeshua (Jesus), and the work of the Holy Spirit. Our aim is not just to give information but to teach Torah principles and demonstrate how to use them in their lives.

Each lesson is designed as a guide for teaching the Torah Portions to children ages 4 to 12 years. This curriculum is filled with creative crafts designed by Yevgeniya and insightful lessons written by Natalee.

Visit our website at www.torah4children.net to learn more about other books from our curriculum and our ministry.

www.ingramcontent.com/pod-product-compliance
Lightning Source LLC
Chambersburg PA
CBHW081331230426
43667CB00018B/2902